SCOTT FORESMAN

Art

TEACHER'S EDITION
Grade K

Robyn Montana Turner, Ph.D.
Program Author

PEARSON

Scott
Foresman

Editorial Offices: Glenview, Illinois • Parsippany, New Jersey • New York, New York

Sales Offices: Needham, Massachusetts • Duluth, Georgia • Glenview, Illinois •
Coppell, Texas • Sacramento, California • Mesa, Arizona

ISBN: 0-328-08039-X
Copyright © 2005, Pearson Education, Inc.
All Rights Reserved. Printed in the United States of America. This publication is protected by Copyright,
and permission should be obtained from the publisher prior to any prohibited reproduction, storage
in a retrieval system, or transmission in any form by any means, electronic, mechanical, photocopying,
recording, or likewise. For information regarding permission(s), write to: Permissions Department,
Scott Foresman, 1900 East Lake Avenue, Glenview, Illinois 60025.

3 4 5 6 7 8 9 10 V064 13 12 11 10 09 08 07 06 05

Kindergarten

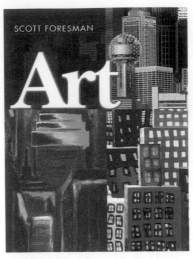

Grade 1

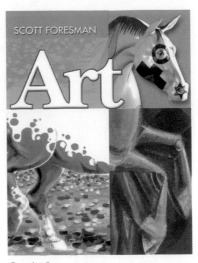

Grade 2

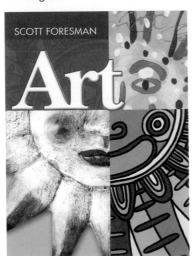

Grade 3

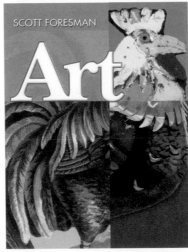

Grade 4

Grade 5

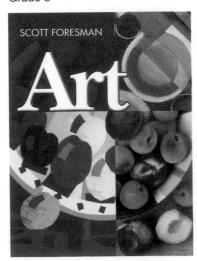

Grade 6

Grade 7

Grade 8

Robyn Montana Turner, Ph.D.

Kindergarten through Grade 6, Austin, Texas

An acclaimed elementary visual arts textbook author, Dr. Turner's visual arts teaching experience spans from pre-kindergarten through graduate school. Most recently, she directed the Visual Arts Student Teacher Program at the University of Texas at Austin. Dr. Turner also conceptualizes and writes trade books for children and young adults. Her award-winning artist biographies, *Portraits of Women Artists for Children,* are featured in libraries and classrooms nationally. Her visual account of the history and culture of Texas, *Texas Traditions: The Culture of the Lone Star State,* received the Teddy Award, the state's highest honor for a children's book. Her academic publications include a chapter in the National Art Education Association anthology *Gender Issues in Art Education,* as well as contributions to the NAEA Journal *Studies in Art Education.*

Rebecca Brooks, Ph.D.

Grades 7 and 8, Austin, Texas

A visual arts and art education professor in the Department of Art and Art History at the University of Texas at Austin, Dr. Brooks is a nationally successful textbook author, lecturer, and researcher, focusing on the development and implementation of interdisciplinary curricula at the elementary, secondary, and college levels. The recipient of two prestigious Foxworth Fellowships from the College of Fine Arts, she received the Texas Art Education Association's Art Educator of the Year for Higher Education (1990) and the National Art Education Association's Art Educator of the Year, Western Division (1991).

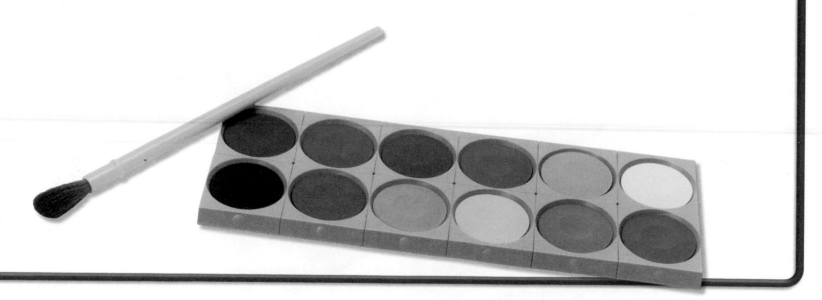

Authors, Consultants & Reviewers

CONTRIBUTING AUTHORS

James M. Clarke, M.Ed.
Grades 6 through 8, Houston, Texas

Executive Director of the Texas Coalition for Quality Arts Education, Mr. Clarke is a successful arts educator, author, consultant, editor, and speaker. The former National Art Education Association and Texas Art Education Association President has won many NAEA honors, including the Marion Quinn Dix Award for Outstanding Leadership. He was on the National Coordinating Board for America's National Standards for Arts Education and a spokesman at the National Education Goals hearings in the 1990s.

Sara A. Chapman, M.Ed.
Grades 6 through 8, Houston, Texas

Coordinator of the Visual Arts Program for Alief Independent School District in Houston, Ms. Chapman is a successful middle school textbook author who has taught all levels of art education, including university course work. Currently Western Region Vice President of the National Art Education Association, she also served as President of the Texas Art Education Association and NAEA. She chaired the Texas Fine Arts Standards Visual Arts team and is a cadre member of the state's Center for Educator Development in the Fine Arts.

PROGRAM CONSULTANTS

Christopher Adejumo, Ph.D.
Associate Professor, Visual Art Studies
University of Texas, Austin, TX

Doug Blandy, Ph.D.
Professor and Director, Arts and Administration Program, Institute for Community Arts and Studies
University of Oregon, Eugene, OR

Rebecca Brooks, Ph.D.
Professor, Department of Art and Art History
University of Texas, Austin, TX

Sara A. Chapman, M.Ed.
Coordinator, Visual Arts Program
Alief Independent School District, Houston, TX

James M. Clarke, M.Ed.
Executive Director, Texas Coalition for Quality Arts Education, Houston, TX

Georgia Collins, Ph.D.
Professor Emeritus, College of Fine Arts
University of Kentucky, Lexington, KY

Deborah Cooper, M.Ed.
Coordinating Director of Arts Education, Curriculum and Instruction
Charlotte-Mecklenburg Schools, Charlotte, NC

Sandra M. Epps, Ph.D.
Multicultural Art Education Consultant
New York, NY

Mary Jo Gardere, B.S.
Multi-Arts Specialist, Eladio Martinez Learning Center
Dallas, TX

Carlos G. Gómez, MFA
Professor of Fine Art, University of Texas at Brownsville and Texas Southmost College, Brownsville, TX

Kristina Lamour, MFA
Assistant Professor, The Art Institute of Boston at Lesley University, Boston, MA

Melinda M. Mayer, Ph.D.
Assistant Professor, School of Visual Arts
University of North Texas, Denton, TX

Robyn Montana Turner, Ph.D.
Author, Austin, TX

CRITIC READERS

Celeste Anderson
Roosevelt Elementary School, Nampa, ID

Mary Jo Birkholz
Wilson Elementary School, Janesville, WI

Mary Jane Cahalan
Mitzi Bond Elementary School, El Paso, TX

Cindy Collar
Cloverleaf Elementary School, Cartersville, GA

Yvonne Days
St. Louis Public Schools, St. Louis, MO

Shirley Dickey
Creative Art Magnet School, Houston, TX

Ray Durkee
Charlotte Performing Arts Center, Punta Gorda, FL

Sue Flores-Minick
Bryker Woods Elementary School, Austin, TX

Denise Jennings
Fulton County Schools, Atlanta, GA

Alicia Lewis
Stevens Elementary School, Houston, TX

James Miller
Margo Elementary School, Weslaco, TX

Marta Olson
Seattle Public Schools, Seattle, WA

Judy Preble
Florence Avenue School, Irvington, NJ

Tonya Roberson
Oleson Elementary School, Houston, TX

Andrew Southwick
Edgewood Independent School District, San Antonio, TX

Nita Ulaszek
Audelia Creek Elementary School, Dallas, TX

Tessie Varthas
Office of Creative and Public Art, Philadelphia, PA

Penelope Venola
Spurgeon Intermediate School, Santa Ana, CA

Elizabeth Willett
Art Specialist, Fort Worth, TX

STUDIO REVIEWERS

Judy Abbott
Art Educator, Allison Elementary School
Austin Independent School District, Austin, TX

Lin Altman
Art Educator, Cedar Creek Elementary School
Eanes Independent School District, Austin, TX

Geral T. Butler
Retired Art Educator, Heritage High School
Lynchburg City Schools, Lynchburg, VA

Dale Case
Elementary Principal, Fox Meadow Elementary School
Nettleton School District, Jonesboro, AR

Deborah McLouth
Art Educator, Zavala Elementary School
Austin Independent School District, Austin, TX

Patricia Newman
Art Educator, Saint Francis Xavier School
Archdiocese of Chicago, La Grange, IL

Nancy Sass
Art Educator, Cambridge Elementary School, Alamo
Heights Independent School District, San Antonio, TX

Sue Spiva Telle
Art Educator, Woodridge Elementary School, Alamo
Heights Independent School District, San Antonio, TX

Cari Washburn
Art Educator, Great Oaks Elementary School, Round
Rock Independent School District, Round Rock, TX

Turn on the power of visual literacy.

Art is a powerful language that ignites imaginations and helps students acquire critical-thinking and communication skills. **Scott Foresman Art** integrates classroom instruction, hands-on activities, and literacy-building experiences to turn on the power of art for all students. **Scott Foresman Art** focuses on the Elements of Art and the Principles of Design, the basic tools artists use to communicate their ideas.

GOOD THINGS HAPPEN WHEN KIDS DO ART!

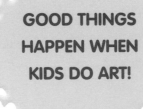

CURRICULUM AND INSTRUCTIONAL ACTIVITIES SUPPORT NATIONAL VISUAL ARTS STANDARDS.

Accessible

- Textbook or fine art system
- Consistent lesson–studio organization
- Readable lessons
- Highlighted vocabulary defined in context with words and images
- Step-by-step studio directions

Relevant

- Motivating content that students can relate to
- ESL Notes in every lesson
- Curriculum Connection in every lesson and on every print
- Meeting Individual Needs in every studio
- Online and CD-ROM technology resources
- Careers in Art unit featured in grades 7 and 8

Teacher Support

- Explicit, easy-to-use lessons
- More than 1,000 transparencies for grades 1 through 8
- Instructional prints support Elements of Art and Principles of Design
- Fine art prints for grades K through 8—24 per grade

Accessible

TEACH FROM THE
Student Edition.

Student Edition: Grade 4

Lesson 1

Color

Colors, or hues, help artists of every culture express their thoughts and feelings. Point to red and blue on the color wheel on page 53. Where do you see these hues in *Geraniums Before Blue Mountain*?

Auguste Macke. *Geraniums Before Blue Mountain,* date unknown. Oil on canvas. 20⅝ by 25⅝ inches. Milwaukee Art Museum. Gift of Mrs. Harry Lynde Bradley.

52

Color Wheel

(intermediate) yellow-green
(primary) yellow
(intermediate) yellow-orange
(secondary) green
(secondary) orange
blue-green (intermediate)
(intermediate) red-orange
blue (primary)
red (primary)
blue-violet (intermediate)
red-violet (intermediate)
violet (secondary)

Point to red, yellow, and blue on the color wheel. They are the **primary colors.** If you mix two primary colors, you get a **secondary color.** Find a secondary color on the color wheel. To make an **intermediate color,** mix a primary color and a secondary color. Look again at Macke's painting. What intermediate colors do you see? Choose one. What hues did Macke mix to get that color?

Sketchbook Journal

Use oil pastels to practice mixing colors. Make some secondary and intermediate hues. Blend colors together with a tissue.

53

HIGHLIGHTED VOCABULARY WORDS

Encourage students to use their new words throughout the day. Defined at point of reference, the highlighted words complement the art images and are easy to find.

SKETCHBOOK JOURNAL

Provide a regular opportunity for students to connect art and writing.

ACCESSIBLE LESSONS AND STUDIOS HELP ALL TEACHERS AND STUDENTS SUCCEED!

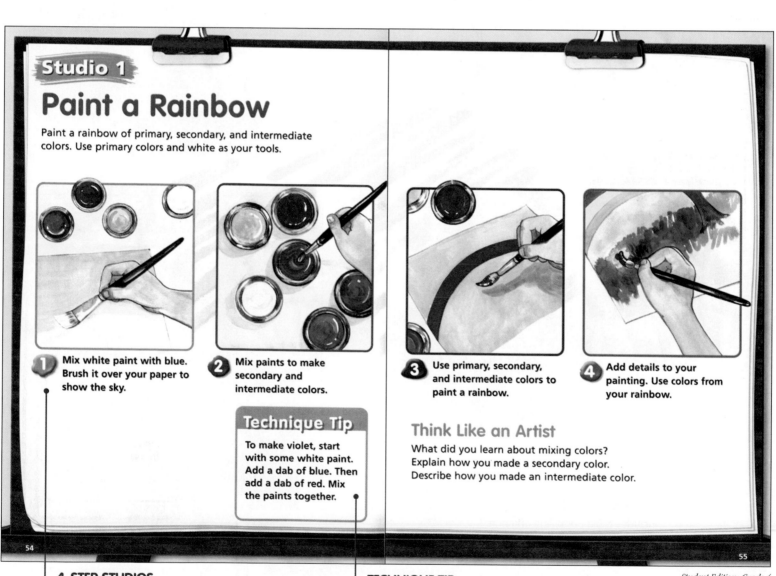

Studio 1

Paint a Rainbow

Paint a rainbow of primary, secondary, and intermediate colors. Use primary colors and white as your tools.

1. Mix white paint with blue. Brush it over your paper to show the sky.

2. Mix paints to make secondary and intermediate colors.

Technique Tip

To make violet, start with some white paint. Add a dab of blue. Then add a dab of red. Mix the paints together.

3. Use primary, secondary, and intermediate colors to paint a rainbow.

4. Add details to your painting. Use colors from your rainbow.

Think Like an Artist

What did you learn about mixing colors? Explain how you made a secondary color. Describe how you made an intermediate color.

54

55

Student Edition: Grade 4

4-STEP STUDIOS

Allow students to think and act like artists by presenting the creative process in simple terms using 4 easy steps—shown by both pictures and words.

TECHNIQUE TIP

Offer ways to connect the process with the results as students follow creative ideas that were created by art teachers.

TEACH FROM THE

Fine Art System.

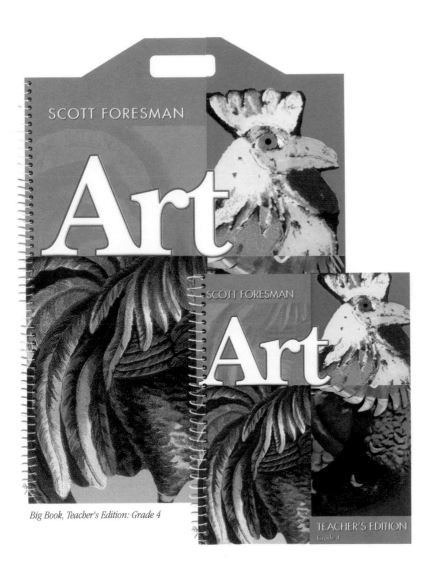

Big Book, Teacher's Edition: Grade 4

FINE ART RESOURCE SYSTEM

Includes a Big Book, fine art prints, easel, Teacher's Edition, fine art transparencies, Unit-by-Unit Resources, Integrated Reading and Writing Workbook with Answer Key, and large binder.

Unit-by-Unit Resources, Integrated Reading and Writing Workbook with Answer Key, Master Index: Grade 3

Fine Art Print and Fine Art Transparency: Grade 3

1988. From the Women on a Bridge Series. Acrylic on canvas with pieced fabric border, 74 by 69 inches. The Solomon R. ...w York. © 1988 Faith Ringgold.

Grade 3: Art Print 1

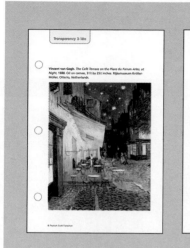

Fine Art Transparencies: Grade 3

FINE ART TRANSPARENCIES

Place your choice of images side by side to provide a compare and contrast discussion among students. Choose from more than 1,000 images for grades 1 through 8.

TEACH ART FOR ART'S SAKE!

Carmen Lomas Garza. *Barbacoa para Cumpleaños (Birthday Barbeque)*, 1993. Alkyds on canvas, 36 by 48 inches. Collection of Federal Reserve Bank of Dallas. © 1993 Carmen Lomas Garza (reg. 1994). Photo by M. Lee Fatherree, courtesy of Carmen Lomas Garza.

Art

Grade 4: Art Print 22

Fine Art Print: Grade 4

FINE ART PRINTS—24 PER GRADE

Find detailed notes about the artist and the artwork plus a Curriculum Connection on the back of each laminated 18" x 24" print. In English and in Spanish.

...t the Artist

...Lomas Garza
...tas, or little
...hat Lomas
...ludes in her
...often rep-
...embers of
...y.

... Lomas
...(born 1948)
...p in rural

...Garza often
...cenes of
...hood,
...g the
...and friends
...de up her
close-knit Chicano
community.

• Lomas Garza's work documents the traditional celebrations and emphasizes the joys of everyday life.

Carmen Lomas Garza
Las *monitas*, pequeñas figuras que la artista incluye en sus pinturas, generalmente representan a personas de su familia.

• Carmen Lomas Garza (nacida en 1948) se crió en Texas, en una zona rural.

• A menudo pinta escenas de su niñez, incluyendo a los familiares y amigos que componían su comunidad chicana.

• Su obra documenta las celebraciones tradicionales y pone énfasis en las alegrías de la vida cotidiana.

...showing a multi-generational group
...picado banner decorations.

...artista: un grupo de personas de varias generaciones, cumpleaños. Hallen las decoraciones de papel picado.

Looking Closely at Art

• Describe where you see diagonal lines. (clothesline, roof, tree branches, position of the tables, direction of the smoke) DESCRIBE

• How did Garza call your attention to the girl at the piñata? (She is surrounded by a circle of people.) ANALYZE

• What does this painting tell you about the family? (Possible answer: Everyone enjoys each other.) INTERPRET

• What part is most interesting to you? Tell why. (Answers will vary.) JUDGE

• Digan dónde ven líneas diagonales. (en la cuerda de tender la ropa, en el techo, en las ramas del árbol, en la posición de las mesas o en la dirección del humo) DESCRIBIR

• ¿De qué manera la artista logra atraer su atención hacia la niña que está junto a la piñata? (La niña está rodeada de gente, que forma un círculo a su alrededor.) ANALIZAR

• ¿Qué les dice esta pintura acerca de la familia? (Respuesta posible: Que todos disfrutan de la compañía de los demás.) INTERPRETAR

• ¿Qué parte les interesa más? ¿Por qué? (Las respuestas variarán.) DAR UNA OPINIÓN

Curriculum Connection

Math
Birthday Celebrations Have students plan a surprise party for the principal. Tell students to record all the supplies they will need, estimate the costs of each item, and calculate the total expenses.

Language Arts
Invitation Have students create an invitation to a party like the one shown in the painting. Discuss what words and graphics make an appealing invitation.

Matemáticas
Fiestas de cumpleaños Pida a los estudiantes que planeen una fiesta sorpresa para el director o la directora de la escuela. Pídales que anoten todo lo que necesitarán para la fiesta, que estimen el costo de cada artículo y que calculen los gastos totales.

Artes del lenguaje
Invitación Pida a los estudiantes que hagan una invitación para una fiesta como la de la pintura. Comenten qué palabras e ilustraciones harían atractiva la invitación.

Art is all around us.

Lesson 1

At a Glance

Objectives

- Identify and describe beauty in natural and constructed environments.
- Describe, analyze, interpret, and judge artworks.

Materials

- **Fine Art Transparency**
- pencil and paper
- Sketchbook Journal

Vocabulary

natural environment, constructed environment, objects, details

NVAS (5–8) #2 Using knowledge of structures and functions

NVAS (5–8) #5 Reflecting upon and assessing the characteristics and merits of their work and the work of others

NVAS (5–8) #6 Making connections between visual arts and other disciplines

❶ Introduce

Have students draw an object in the classroom that they think is beautiful. Ask students to emphasize what makes it pleasing.

Then ask students to describe, as thoroughly as possible, what makes the object beautiful. Prompt them to use words that describe how the object looks and feels. As students give the verbal details, encourage them to add the visual representation of those details to their sketches. Refer students to the photographs in the lesson, and ask them to describe the details they see in the close-up images.

18

Lesson 1

Beauty in Your World

Beauty surrounds you. You can find beauty in the **natural environment,** such as plants, rocks, and sky. You can also discover beauty in the **constructed environment.** These are the things or **objects** made by humans, such as buildings and artworks. Take a closer look at objects you see in your environments. What makes each object beautiful?

This photograph shows a natural environment. What does your natural environment look like?

Filippo Brunelleschi. *Dome of the Florence Cathedral,* 1420–1436. Florence, Italy.

You can also discover beauty by noticing **details.** These are small parts that make up a whole. Where do you see details on these pages? Details can help you notice the elements of art in objects and artworks. They can also help you find beauty in everyday objects in your environment.

Sketchbook Journal

Focus on the beauty found in your natural and constructed environments. Draw details of objects of beauty. Label the details that make them pleasing.

18   19

🎨 Art Background

About the Artist Italian Filippo Brunelleschi (1377–1446), who designed the dome that covers the Florence Cathedral, developed a mathematical technique for perspective in two-dimensional artworks. By using parallel lines converging to a vanishing point, artists created the illusion of three dimensions.

ESL Notes

Have students look through images in magazines and identify examples of natural and constructed environments. Encourage students to name the terms they identify.

🧩 Curriculum Connection

Math Students can explore the Golden Ratio in constructed and natural environments. The Golden Ratio is approximately 1.618:1.

If students measure the height and width of the face in Leonardo da Vinci's *Mona Lisa,* they will find that the numbers reflect the Golden Ratio. The same is true for the length and width of the Parthenon.

Encourage students to look for other examples of the Golden Ratio in art and nature by taking measurements to prove the relationship.

NATIONAL VISUAL ARTS STANDARDS

Discover at a glance how lesson skills correlate to national standards.

ESL NOTES

Offer additional instructional strategies for ESL students or those who need greater help in understanding the lesson concept. In every lesson.

CURRICULUM CONNECTION

Introduce activities that help students relate art to other disciplines. All disciplines are represented throughout the course.

THE FELDMAN MODEL OF ART CRITIQUE

Use an easy 4-step process of art critique (describe, analyze, interpret, judge) in every lesson to develop higher-order thinking skills.

② Teach

Have students read pages 18–19 and the credit line. Tell students to look closely at the dome on page 19. Ask:

- **Is this an example of a constructed or natural environment?** (constructed environment) DESCRIBE
- **What does the smaller photograph allow you to see that the larger one does not?** (The detail of the top of the dome.) ANALYZE
- **What does the size of the dome tell you about it?** (Possible response: It is the biggest part of the building; it is important) INTERPRET
- **What part of the dome is most interesting to you? Why?** (Possible response: the lines in the dome; because it brings my eye to the top) JUDGE

Sketchbook Journal Encourage students to pay attention to elements such as texture, value, and space, as well as form and color.

③ Close

Have students share their images from the Sketchbook Journal with a partner and point out the most appealing details.

Assessment Ask volunteers to describe the images that they drew in their Sketchbook Journal. Students should identify the objects as part of natural or constructed environments, then point out the details that they felt were eye-catching.

Quick Studio
Have students scan still photographs of a character in action and manipulate them to create an animation.

Look for a Quick Studio on the Studio page that follows each lesson.

LOOK AND COMPARE

Develop your students' appreciation for diverse art styles by comparing and contrasting different works of art. Use with graphic organizers.

ARTIST AT WORK (Grades K–6)
MEET THE ARTIST (Grades 7–8)

Help students relate art to the real world by sharing the experiences of artists and their careers.

GRADES 7 & 8
COMPLETE CAREER UNIT

UNIT OPENER

Use motivating and engaging fine art as a springboard for discussions and language-building activities.

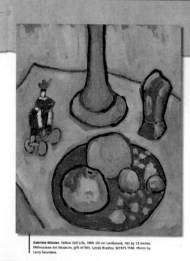

TECHNOLOGY

Support lessons and studios throughout each unit interactively— both online and with CD-ROMs.

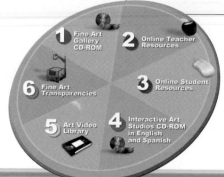

1 Fine Art Gallery CD-ROM
2 Online Teacher Resources
3 Online Student Resources
4 Interactive Art Studios CD-ROM in English and Spanish
5 Art Video Library
6 Fine Art Transparencies

Materials that inspire!

STUDENT EDITION

Grades 1 through 8

- Places fine art and engaging text in students' hands

- Explores a wide range of styles and media

- Exposes students to art and artists in every lesson

- Features readable text

BIG BOOK

Kindergarten through Grade 5

- Student book pages on a larger scale

- Suitable for whole-class instruction

- Great display for center or small-group activities

TEACHER'S EDITION

Kindergarten through Grade 8

- Detailed overviews for flexible and easy planning

- Cross-curricular links to core disciplines

- Varied assessment options

FINE ART TRANSPARENCIES

Grades 1 through 8

- More than 1,000 images; most of the fine artworks in the program

- Ideal for compare and contrast discussions

Big Book: Grade 4

Teacher's Edition: Grade 4

Student Edition: Grade 4

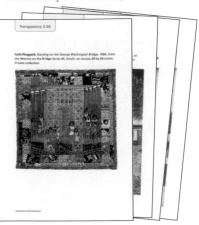

Fine Art Transparencies: Grade 3

OUR CURRICULUM SUPPORTS BOTH CLASSROOM TEACHERS AND ART SPECIALISTS.

FINE ART PRINTS*
Kindergarten through Grade 8

- Laminated 18" x 24" prints

- Instruction and activities in English and in Spanish on the back

- 24 per grade level

INSTRUCTIONAL PRINTS*
Kindergarten through Grade 8

- 16 colorful classroom posters per set with English and Spanish instruction on the back. Includes one poster for each element of art and principle of design and one classroom safety poster (available in English and in Spanish)

- Grade-level sets: Kindergarten through Grade 2, Grade 3 through Grade 5, and Grade 6 through Grade 8

TECHNOLOGY

- Fine Art Gallery Builder CD-ROM (Grades 1 through 8)

- Interactive Studio CD-ROM in English and Spanish (Grades K through 8)

- Scott Foresman SuccessNet online resources include student studios and teacher lesson planner (Grades K through 8)

*Includes Spanish instructional support

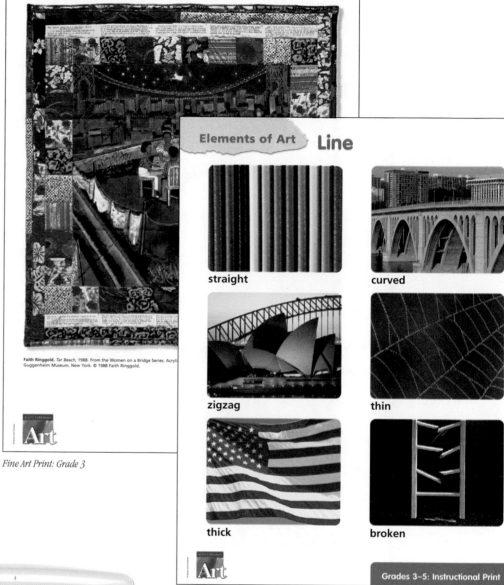

Faith Ringgold. *Tar Beach*, 1988. From the Women on a Bridge Series. Acrylic Guggenheim Museum, New York. © 1988 Faith Ringgold.

Fine Art Print: Grade 3

Elements of Art Line

straight · curved · zigzag · thin · thick · broken

Grades 3–5: Instructional Print

Instructional Print: Grades 3–5

ALSO AVAILABLE:

Unit-by-Unit Resources*
(Kindergarten through Grade 8)

Time Line of Art History

Master Index

Integrated Reading and Writing Workbook and Answer Key*
(Grades 1 through 8)

Contents

Unit 1

Art in My World 16

Marc Chagall. *Green Violinist,* 1923–1924.

Unit 2

Art Nearby. **38**

Gabriele Münter. *Child with Ball*, ca. 1916.

Artist unknown.
Bottle Cap Giraffe,
1966.

2

Unit 4

A World of Art 82

Andy Goldsworthy.
Rain Shadow, 1993.

3

Unit 5

Artists Explore 104

Shields Landon Jones.
Three Musicians, 1975–1978.

4

Unit 6

Michael Moss.
Rocking Chair, 1993.

5

Start with Art

Start with Art

You are an artist.

Your friends are artists too.

Artists make art.

At a Glance

Objectives

- Identify art as a form of expression.
- Understand that art is everywhere in the environment.
- Generate ideas for art.

Vocabulary

artworks

NVAS (K–4) #3 Choosing and evaluating a range of subject matter, symbols, and ideas

NVAS (K–4) #5 Reflecting upon and assessing the characteristics and merits of their work and the work of others

Introduce

Tell children that art is everywhere. Relate art to everyday life by drawing their attention to several artworks in the classroom. Point out that art is more than just paintings and drawings. Explain that furniture, jewelry, and items from everyday life can also be artworks.

As you point out different objects and artworks in the classroom environment, explain to children that they can be described in many ways. Artworks have a variety of colors, textures, forms, and subjects. Identify and comment on examples of each. Ask children to identify examples in other artworks in the classroom.

Then direct children's attention to the child-made artwork on page 6. Model how to express ideas about original artworks by peers by asking yourself questions aloud as you view the artwork. For example, ask:

- **What colors do I see?** (yellow, red, blue)
- **What kind of artwork is this?** (fingerpainting)
- **What does this artwork show?** (sun, flowers)

 Notes

English language learners who have difficulty learning art terms such as *color, texture, form,* and *subject* can benefit from additional examples. Sit with the ESL child and scan artworks printed in the Student Edition for examples of each term.

Works of art are called artworks.

Look all around you.

Where do you see artworks?

ONLY YOU

CAN PREVENT FOREST FIRES

Billboard advertisements can be art.

7

Explore

Tell children that artists use their five senses to glean information from their environment. By identifying the colors, textures, forms, and subjects in the world around them, artists come up with ideas for artworks.

Lead children in identifying subjects in the artworks on page 7. Refer to the Nigerian sculpture. Ask: **What do you see?** (a rooster) Explain that the artist probably chose a rooster as the subject of the artwork after seeing roosters in the environment.

Direct children's attention to the billboard. Ask: **What do you see in this billboard?** (Smokey the Bear) Ask children to describe other billboards they have seen.

Develop Ideas for Artworks Mention several animals you have seen, such as cats, hamsters, dogs, and so on. Choose an animal as the one you would like to show in an artwork. Ask children to brainstorm other subjects from their environments that might make interesting subjects for artworks.

Close

Ask children to name a scene or object they would like to show in an artwork. Have them tell what ideas or feelings they would express through the artwork.

Your Art Words

At a Glance

Objectives

- Identify the elements of art and the principles of design.

Vocabulary

line, space, form, texture, shape, value, color, emphasis, proportion, variety, pattern, rhythm, balance, unity

NVAS (K–4) #5 Reflecting upon and assessing the characteristics and merits of their work and the work of others

Introduce

Play I Spy with children. Have them point to a straight line in the classroom. For example, say: **I spy a straight line.** After you initially point to the straight line, then have children point to other examples. Continue naming other vocabulary words and have children point to examples in the classroom.

Read pages 8–9 to children. Explain that they will learn these and many other art words. Tell children that these words can describe objects and artworks in their environment.

Your Art Words

Your book has many art words.

You will see them in **yellow.**

Artists use art words to talk about art.

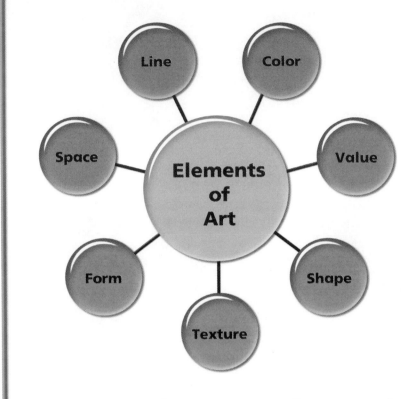

These art words name parts of an artwork.

8

 Notes

Provide pictures and tactile objects to help children better understand the art words and concepts as you go through the units. For example, as you identify and describe colors, display a variety of materials that share the same color. After repeating the color name several times, provide ample opportunities for children to identify the color and say its name.

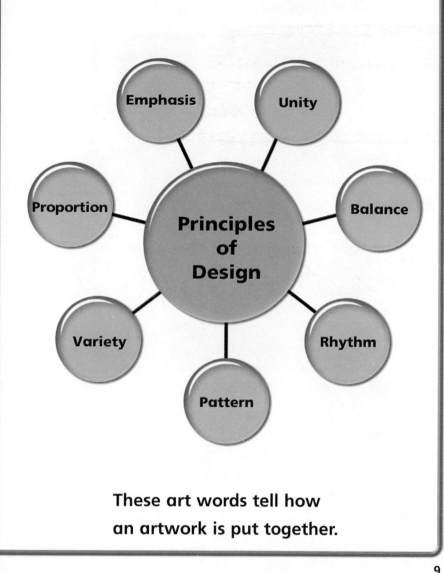

These art words tell how
an artwork is put together.

9

Explore

Tell children that art words help us talk about artworks created by peers and others. Model using the words on pages 8–9 to describe a child's artwork from a previous class, one of your own artworks, or an **Art Print**. Comment on color, shape, line, and so on. Say:

- **I see many different lines. Who can point to a line in this artwork? Describe it.**
- **What is your favorite color? Did the artist use this color?**
- **What shapes do you see? Where else have you seen these shapes?**

Close

Ask children to talk about elements of art or principles of design they will consider as they create future artworks. Prompt them to use words listed on pages 8 and 9.

 Meeting Individual Needs

Reteach Display fabric samples cut into different shapes and sizes to help children who have difficulty understanding some of the art words. Choose cloth with bright primary colors or with bold lines and patterns. Include textured textiles such as corduroy and velour. Guide students as they use art words to describe the fabric samples.

Visit a Museum

At a Glance

Objectives

• Explore the role of art museums.

NVAS (K–4) # 5 Reflecting upon and assessing the characteristics and merits of their work and the work of others

Introduce

After reading aloud the text on page 11, initiate a discussion about art exhibitions and museums. Ask: **Have any of you ever visited an art museum?**

Invite children who have visited a museum to share their experiences, or share your own experiences. Point out that artworks often look very different in person than they do in books. For example, viewers may note these differences:

• Brush strokes might be visible on a painting.
• Fingerprints might show on a clay sculpture.
• The actual size of an artwork might be much bigger or much smaller than expected.

Direct children's attention to the painting on page 10. Then ask them if they think the artwork is bigger or smaller in real life. (Answers will vary. The painting is much larger than it appears on this page.)

Jean-Baptiste-Siméon Chardin. *Soap Bubbles*, probably 1733/1734. Oil on canvas, 36⅝ by 29⅝ inches. National Gallery of Art, Washington, D.C.

Career Research

Guest Speaker Ask a museum curator or docent to speak to your class. Work with children to prepare questions for the guest speaker ahead of time. Ask the speaker to discuss what he or she does in terms of taking care of and displaying artworks.

Field Trip Take children to see an art exhibition. If there is not a local museum, explore alternative exhibition spaces, such as a community building or a gallery. Be sure to get permission first. Schedule the visit during off-peak hours to avoid disrupting business. Allow time for children to express ideas about the exhibition. Model by saying: **This exhibition shows artworks by a variety of artists. I enjoy seeing different types of artworks, such as drawings, paintings, and sculptures.**

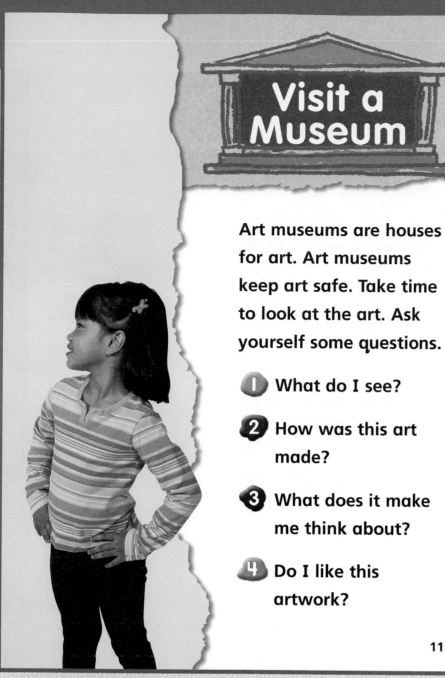

Visit a Museum

Art museums are houses for art. Art museums keep art safe. Take time to look at the art. Ask yourself some questions.

1 What do I see?

2 How was this art made?

3 What does it make me think about?

4 Do I like this artwork?

11

 Gallery Options

Classroom Exhibition Help children learn to express ideas about original artworks by peers by holding a class art exhibition. Choose and display several child-made artworks in your classroom. Before children view the artworks, help them brainstorm three or four questions to ask themselves as they look. Encourage them to show respect for differing opinions.

Explore

Explain to children that asking questions about an artwork can help them better understand it. Direct their attention to the painting on page 10. Use the bulleted questions and answers to model for children how to identify simple subjects expressed in artworks and how to express ideas about original artworks.

- **What does this picture show?** (A young man blowing bubbles.)
- **How did the artist make it?** (He painted it.)
- **What is the most important part of the painting?** (The young man's face.)
- **What do I like best?** (The shape of the bubble.)

Invite children to share their own ideas about the artwork. Tell children that oftentimes there will be others who have differing opinions than they do. Remind them to be respectful of the opinions of others. Point out that in order to show respect, they should remain calm and let each child finish talking.

Museum Etiquette

Tell students to follow these rules when viewing art in a museum or classroom.

- Whisper so you do not disturb others.
- Never touch artworks.
- Try not to walk in front of people who are looking at an artwork.
- Never take food or drinks into a museum or gallery.

Close

Have students state in their own words what a museum is and why they might like to go to see artworks in a museum.

Art Tools

Art Tools

At a Glance

Objectives

• Understand how to use a variety of art tools.
• Assemble a portfolio.

Materials

• Various art materials as shown on Student Edition page 12
• construction paper
• glue
• crayons, markers, and other art tools and materials

NVAS (K–4) # 1 Understanding and applying media, techniques, and processes

NVAS (K–4) # 3 Choosing and evaluating a range of subject matter, symbols, and ideas

NVAS (K–4) # 5 Reflecting upon and assessing the characteristics and merits of their work and the work of others

Introduce

Gather a variety of art tools similar to those pictured on page 12. Tell children that these and many other art tools will help them make drawings, paintings, and other artworks. Ask: **What art tools have you used?**

Name each art tool and discuss the different types of artworks that artists make with each. Encourage children to handle the tools by passing them around.

Model for children how to use a variety of art tools. For example, show how different art tools produce different results by drawing lines with crayons, markers, and paint. Encourage children to practice using the art tools. Ask: **What art tools would you like to use? How would you use them?**

Art Tools

Artists use art tools.

Which ones can you name?

These tools are used for drawing.

These tools are used for painting.

These tools are used for cutting, taping, and pasting.

These tools are used for working with clay.

This tool is used for taking pictures.

12

 Home Connection

Have children ask their parents or caregivers to look around the house for items that can be used as art tools. In addition to paper and pencils, they might find, for example, plastic knives that can be used to model clay. Encourage children to make artworks at home using these tools and share them with the class.

Make a Portfolio

Artists often keep their artworks in a portfolio.

1 Get paper.

2 Glue the paper.

3 Draw.

4 Decorate.

13

![people icon] **Meeting Individual Needs**

Inclusion You may find that many children do not have the fine-motor skills to manipulate many of the art tools listed. Provide opportunities throughout the year for children to practice manipulating different utensils and materials. You will note that many children will be able to handle the art tools much more effectively by the end of the year.

Explore

Make a Portfolio Tell children that they are going to make a portfolio, or folder. They will use their new portfolios to store and protect their artworks. Explain that keeping a portfolio also allows artists to see how their artworks change and develop over time.

Review the steps for making a portfolio, then distribute materials. As children apply personal designs to their portfolios, encourage them to experiment with as many of the art tools shown on page 12 as possible.

Analyze Portfolios After students finish their portfolios, tell them that they have just created an artwork. Ask them to share their ideas about their personal artworks with the rest of the class. Show children a portfolio that you made. Model how to express ideas about it by making comments such as, **I like how I was able to use crayons, markers, and paints in the same artwork. I also like how the colors look together.**

Lead the class in a discussion of each artwork. Remind children to be respectful of the artist and of differing opinions.

Finally, point out to children that throughout the year they will have similar discussions about a wide variety of artworks in portfolios and exhibitions by peers and professional artists.

Close

Have students name an art tool and tell what kinds of artworks an artist might create with it.

Sketchbook Journal

At a Glance

Objectives

- Create a personal Sketchbook Journal.
- Develop and organize ideas from the environment.

Materials

- drawing paper
- paper punch
- yarn
- crayons, markers, and other art tools and materials

NVAS (K–4) #1 Understanding and applying media, techniques, and processes

NVAS (K–4) #2 Using knowledge of structures and functions

NVAS (K–4) #3 Choosing and evaluating a range of subject matter, symbols, and ideas

Introduce

Explain to children that they will use their Sketchbook Journals to draw things they have seen. Direct their attention to the artwork on page 14. Ask: **What did the artist draw?** (a woman)

Tell children that they can also use their Sketchbook Journals to draw images they invent. Then model for children how to create an artwork using a variety of colors, forms, and lines in an invented image. For instance, show children an object with a geometric form, such as a ball or cube. Draw the form on an overhead transparency. Place the transparency on the projector. Add lines and circles to the form to create an imaginary animal. Then add color to the animal.

Make a Sketchbook Journal

A sketchbook is an art tool.

Artists write and draw in it.

Mary Cassatt. *Study for At the Opera,* ca. 1879. Graphite pencil on paper, 4 by 6 inches. Museum of Fine Arts, Boston, MA. Gift of Dr. Hans Schaeffer, 55.28. Photograph © 2003 Museum of Fine Arts, Boston.

14

 ESL Notes

Tell children that when they come across a new word, they should copy it into their Sketchbook Journals. Show them how to draw or color beside each word to help them remember its meaning. For example, beside the words *red, blue,* and *yellow,* use a crayon to make a circle in the appropriate color.

Follow these steps to make
your own Sketchbook Journal.

① **Fold.**

② **Make holes.**

③ **Lace and tie.**

④ **Decorate.**

15

Inclusion Offer children alternative approaches to creating their portfolios and Sketchbook Journals. For example, children having difficulty gluing their portfolios can use tape. You may prefer to have them use manila folders or large envelopes. Children having difficulty binding their Sketchbook Journals may find more success using a loose-leaf binder or a spiral notebook. Whatever materials or products the children use, encourage them to add their own personal designs.

Explore

Explain to children that artists practice using all of their senses when they write and draw in their Sketchbook Journals. Say: **As you begin drawing, remember to look around for things to draw and ideas for how you will draw them. Listen for sounds and think about how things feel and smell. Sometimes you can even taste objects in your environment, like foods.**

Bring three different fruits to class to model how artists use all of their senses to observe. Describe how each piece of fruit looks, feels, smells, and tastes. Say: **An artist uses all this information to create a drawing or printing or other kind of artwork.**

Ask children to remember a special occasion, such as a birthday or holiday celebration. Help them recall sensory details. What things did they see? What sounds did they hear? What aromas did they smell? What did the food taste like? What did the decorations feel like? Say: **All of this information can inspire you to create many kinds of artworks and give you ideas for how to make them.**

Close

Have children display their Sketchbook Journals for their classmates. Ask artists to comment on how they used their senses to create the decoration on the cover of their Sketchbook Journals.

Unit 1 Overview

Art can be found everywhere. It can be discovered in everyday objects as well as in galleries and museums. In this unit, children will learn about artworks and the people who make them. They will also create their own artworks using the elements of art and principles of design.

	Unit Opener, p. 16	Lesson 1, p. 18 **Art Is Everywhere** **Studio 1, p. 19** **Make Hands-on Art**	Lesson 2, p. 20 **Line** **Studio 2, p. 21** **Draw Lines**	Lesson 3, p. 22 **Shape** **Studio 3, p. 23** **Paste Shapes**	Look and Compare, p. 24 **Animals in Art**
Artworks	**Albrecht Dürer.** *Hare,* 1502.		**Utagawa Kuniyoshi.** *Study of a Cat,* date unknown.	**Henri Matisse.** *Ivy in Flower,* 1953.	**Albrecht Dürer.** *Screech Owl,* 1508. **Betty Parsons.** *Winged Frog,* 1978.
Vocabulary		art	artist, lines	shapes	
Materials	• **Art Print 1** • **Instructional Prints** • art tools (crayons, paintbrush, etc.)	• art tools (crayons, paintbrush, glue, etc.) • bag, finger paints, finger paint paper, sponges, smocks	• masking tape, drawing paper, black crayons	• colored paper shapes, construction paper, paste, damp paper towels	**Art Prints 1, 2, 3**
Connections	**Home Connection** artworks at home **Bookshelf** *I Spy Treasure Hunt: A Book of Picture Riddles* by Jean Marzollo, Cartwheel Books (Scholastic), 1999	**Visual Culture** choices in art **ESL Notes** **Fine Arts Connection** Dance: shape and line movements **Meeting Individual Needs** Reteach	**ESL Notes** **Curriculum Connection** Science: lines in natural objects **Meeting Individual Needs** Extend	**ESL Notes** **Curriculum Connection** Math: lines and shapes **Meeting Individual Needs** Extend	**Reading Strategy** Use graphic organizers
Assessment Opportunities		Rubric 1 from **Unit-by-Unit Resources** Ongoing Assessment	Rubric 1 from **Unit-by-Unit Resources** Ongoing Assessment	Rubric 1 from **Unit-by-Unit Resources** Ongoing Assessment	

Lesson 4, p. 26 Senses **Studio 4, p. 27** **Use Your Senses**	Lesson 5, p. 28 Color **Studio 5, p. 29** **Draw with Colors**	Lesson 6, p. 30 Warm and Cool Colors **Studio 6, p. 31** **Color Feelings**	Artist at Work, p. 32 Picture Books	Portfolio Project, p. 34 Draw Yourself	Unit Review, p. 36
Carmen Lomas Garza. *Empanadas*, 1991.	**Marc Chagall.** *Green Violinist*, 1923–1924.	**Pablo Picasso.** *Child with a Dove*, 1901.	**Lois Ehlert.** *Color Zoo.*		**Joan Miró.** Illustration for the book, *Talking Alone*, 1948.
senses	colors	warm colors, cool colors	illustrations		
• old magazines, scissors ⚠, glue, crayons, construction paper, trays	• bag, objects that are one color, crayons, white drawing paper	• crayons, white drawing paper	• picture books • Sketchbook Journals	• Sketchbook Journals • crayons or markers, scissors ⚠, colored construction paper, large drawing paper, paste or glue	• **Art Print 4** • children's art portfolios
Technology Make a poster **ESL Notes** **Meeting Individual Needs** Inclusion	**ESL Notes** **Fine Arts Connection** Music: stringed instruments **Meeting Individual Needs** Extend	**ESL Notes** **Curriculum Connection** Social Studies: strong feelings **Meeting Individual Needs** Reteach	**Career Research** People who illustrate picture books **Reading Strategy** Use prior knowledge	**Gallery Options** Classroom portrait gallery **Meeting Individual Needs** Reteach	
Rubric 1 from **Unit-by-Unit Resources** Ongoing Assessment	Rubric 1 from **Unit-by-Unit Resources** Ongoing Assessment	Rubric 1 from **Unit-by-Unit Resources** Ongoing Assessment		Rubric 1 from **Unit-by-Unit Resources**	**Unit-by-Unit Resources** Vocabulary Worksheets, pp. 11–14 Unit 1 Test, pp. 19–22

Unit 1

At a Glance

Objectives

- Identify the elements of art in artworks.
- Relate art to personal experiences.
- Respond to and make judgments about artworks.

Materials

- **Art Print 1**
- art tools (crayons, paintbrushes, etc.)

NVAS (K–4) #4 Understanding the visual arts in relation to history and cultures

NVAS (K–4) #6 Making connections between visual arts and other disciplines

Introduce the Unit

Ask children to listen and watch as you perform the finger play "My Hare." Create actions to suit the words on page 17. Repeat several times, encouraging children to join in. Explain that a hare is like a rabbit, but it has larger ears and longer hind feet.

Point to *Hare* and tell children that this painting is an example of the hare they heard about in the finger play. Have children express ideas about this painting by Dürer. Model by saying: **I like this painting of a hare. It looks like a real animal.** Then ask:

- **Where are the hare's long fuzzy ears? How do you know they are fuzzy?** (Possible response: because the artist drew fur on them)
- **What are some other parts of the hare that you see? Tell about them.** (Possible responses: brown nose, sharp claws, dark eyes, soft fur, long whiskers)

Albrecht Dürer. *Hare*, 1502. Watercolor, 9¾ by 8¼ inches. Graphische Sammlung Albertina, Vienna, Austria. Erich Lessing/Art Resource, NY.

16

 Art Background

Hare In this highly realistic watercolor, Albrecht Dürer (1471–1528) exhibits his talent that made him a great German Renaissance painter. The hare appears to be turning its silky ears toward a sound while it sits very still. Its bright eyes, sharp claws, and the finely detailed hairs of its fur help bring the artwork to life.

 Home Connection

Suggest to children that they ask a family member to find artworks at home that the children did when they were younger. Children can share the items and tell about themselves as artists.

Art in My World

My Hare

Long fuzzy ears

And a soft brown nose,

My little hare hops

Wherever she goes!

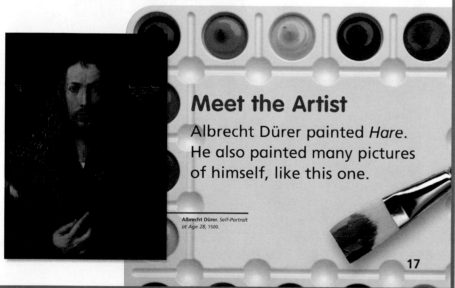

Meet the Artist

Albrecht Dürer painted *Hare*. He also painted many pictures of himself, like this one.

Albrecht Dürer. *Self-Portrait at Age 28*, 1500.

17

Bookshelf

I Spy Treasure Hunt: A Book of Picture Riddles
by Jean Marzollo
Cartwheel Books (Scholastic), 1999

This book is one in a popular series that uses rhyme, interesting objects, and artfully arranged photographs to encourage children to really look at what is around them.

Discuss Unit Concepts

Point to the self-portrait of Albrecht Dürer and ask children who they think is the subject of this painting. Tell children to look at the person's clothes and hair for clues. (the artist who painted *Hare*) Read the information about him and encourage children to speculate why his hair and clothing look so different. (Possible response: He lived long ago, in a different country.)

Explain that this artist lived and worked four hundred years ago, long before there were cameras, movies, or computers. People used art to show what they saw around them. Tell children that in this unit, they are going to learn about *artworks*—objects and pictures made by people— and create some of their own.

As you introduce each element of art and principle of design in Unit 1, you may wish to display the **Instructional Prints.** A print is provided for each element and principle.

Meet the Artist

Albrecht Dürer (1471–1528) Albrecht Dürer was a German painter and engraver. From a young age he showed an amazing gift for drawing, and as was usual in his day, he was apprenticed to a master artist in Nuremberg, Germany. Although known for his many religious artworks, Dürer also completed several studies of plants and animals with his characteristic attention to texture, form, and detail.

Lesson 1

At a Glance

Objectives

• Identify and describe art in the environment.
• Use finger paint to make lines.
• Respond to and make judgments about artworks.

Materials

• art tools (crayons, paintbrush, glue, etc.)
• bag, finger paints, finger paint paper, sponges, smocks
• Rubric 1 from **Unit-by-Unit Resources**

Vocabulary

art

NVAS (K–4) #1 Understanding and applying media, techniques, and processes
NVAS (K–4) #2 Using knowledge of structures and functions
NVAS (K–4) #3 Choosing and evaluating a range of subject matter, symbols, and ideas
NVAS (K–4) #6 Making connections between visual arts and other disciplines

❶ Teach

Display examples of children's art. Invite the children who made the artworks to tell how they made them, and why.

Display page 18 and talk about the boy who is painting. Point out additional information about the photograph, such as the colorful artworks behind him. Then give children time to describe what they see in the photograph. After you read the page aloud, explain that everyone can make art. Ask:

• **Would you like to be the boy in the photograph? Why or why not?** (Possible response: Yes, because I like messy things.)

Art Is Everywhere

Art is made by people.
You can make art.
What do you like to make?

18

 Visual Culture

Tell children that art is fun. Ask them why they think the photograph on page 18 is a good choice, or not a good choice, to say visually that art is fun. (Possible response: It is a good choice because the boy looks as if he is having fun.)

ESL Notes

Help children learn words for feelings. Smile as you point to the boy on page 18 and say: **He is happy.** Encourage children to repeat the sentence as they point to the boy. Point to yourself, smile, and say: **I am happy.** Invite children to chant or sing the sentence several times.

Make Hands-on Art

Studio 1

1. **Wipe.**
2. **Pick a color.**
3. **Touch.**
4. **Finger paint!**

Art in My World

Find artworks in your classroom.

19

② Create

Invite children to look at the pictures as you point to and read the steps. Ask children who have finger painted before to describe their experiences.

Be sure to use glossy paper so that the finger paint is not absorbed into the paper. Have children wet the entire paper first so that the paint flows smoothly across the surface.

Technique Tip Show children that they can make different kinds of lines using different parts of their hands. For example, fingernails make sharp, thin lines and knuckles make broad lines with rounded edges.

Quick Studio Create an art center space for children to take turns finger painting on a tabletop. When one group is done, tell them to leave the paint on the table for the next group.

③ Close

Use the *Art in My World* prompt to help children glean information from the environment using their senses.

Ongoing Assessment

If . . . children have trouble covering their entire paper with paint,

then . . . suggest that they wet the parts of the paper that are too dry, or add more paint.

See page 18 from **Unit-by-Unit Resources** for a rubric to assess this studio.

 Fine Arts Connection

Dance Give each child a scarf or a crepe-paper streamer. Play dance music with a slow, calming tempo. Ask children to make movements that resemble the shapes and lines they made with the finger paints.

 Meeting Individual Needs

Reteach Some children may be reluctant to "get messy." Do not force them to participate, but do encourage them to listen and watch as other children finger paint. You might suggest that they use just the tip of their two index fingers to begin.

Lesson 2

At a Glance

Objectives

• Identify and describe lines in artworks.
• Use black crayons to draw a variety of lines.
• Respond to and make judgments about artworks.

Materials

• masking tape, drawing paper, black crayons
• Rubric 1 from **Unit-by-Unit Resources**

Vocabulary

artist, lines

NVAS (K–4) #1 Understanding and applying media, techniques, and processes
NVAS (K–4) #2 Using knowledge of structures and functions
NVAS (K–4) #3 Choosing and evaluating a range of subject matter, symbols, and ideas

❶ Teach

Use masking tape to make lines on the floor. As children walk along each line, describe it—curved, thin, straight, etc.

Display page 20 and read the page aloud. Explain that an artist is a person who creates art. Tell children that a line can be a mark made by a pencil, crayon, or other tool. Then describe what you see in the drawing. Model how to express ideas about the drawing by saying: **The artist of this drawing used straight, curved, thin, and thick lines. These different lines make the cat look like it is looking out the corner of its eye.** Then give children time to share their ideas. Ask:

• **Is it a fat cat or a skinny cat?** (fat) **How do you know?** (curved lines to make its body)

Lesson 2

Line

An artist drew this cat.
He used curved **lines.**
Where is the cat looking?

Utagawa Kuniyoshi. *Study of a Cat,* date unknown. From Kuniyoshi's sketchbook. ©The Board of Trustees, Victoria & Albert Museum, London/Art Resource, NY.

20

 Art Background

About the Artist Utagawa Kuniyoshi (1798–1861) was a Japanese painter and printmaker. He engraved pictures on wood blocks and then printed them in various colors. His subjects included landscapes, actors, animals, and episodes from Japanese history. He is reputed to have loved cats, having at least ten of them in his home at one time.

ESL Notes

Draw a thin line and a thick line on the board. As you point to a line, say: **This line is thin (thick).** Encourage children to repeat the sentence as they point to the line. Repeat with other lines and describing words, such as **long, straight,** and **curved.**

Draw Lines

1 **Choose.**

2 **Draw.**

3 **Share.**

4 **Work together.**

Think Like an Artist

Which line is your favorite? Why?

21

Curriculum Connection

Science Display a variety of natural objects, such as leaves, shells, twigs, and rocks. Invite children to find as many lines as they can in the objects, using hand lenses if possible. They can record what they see in their Sketchbook Journals.

Meeting Individual Needs

Extend Invite children to cover their paper with vertical lines, using a light-colored crayon. They can use darker crayons to draw other types of lines across the vertical lines.

2 Create

Invite children to look at the pictures as you point to and read the steps. Identify and describe the kinds of lines they will make on their paper.

In Steps 3 and 4, have children choose partners. They can share ideas for kinds of lines to draw.

Technique Tip Point out the short, soft lines that Kuniyoshi used to suggest the cat's fur. Have children experiment with their crayons to show how different things might feel. For example, they might draw with the tip of the crayon to make soft, broad strokes of color.

Quick Studio Have partners work together to create different lines. You can have them work at the chalkboard or on large paper.

3 Close

Create a drawing. Use it to model expressing ideas about a personal artwork. Then have children use the *Think Like an Artist* questions to reflect on their own work. (Possible response: I like zigzag lines because they are fun to make and interesting to look at.)

Ongoing Assessment

If . . . children have trouble making a variety of lines,

then . . . model drawing a variety of lines on the chalkboard or in the air. Invite children to try some on their own.

See page 18 from **Unit-by-Unit Resources** for a rubric to assess this studio.

Lesson 3

At a Glance

Objectives

- Identify and describe shapes in artworks.
- Arrange a variety of shapes in a cut-paper collage.
- Respond to and make judgments about artworks.

Materials

- colored paper shapes, construction paper, paste, damp paper towels
- Rubric 1 from **Unit-by-Unit Resources**

Vocabulary

shapes

NVAS (K–4) #1 Understanding and applying media, techniques, and processes

NVAS (K–4) #2 Using knowledge of structures and functions

NVAS (K–4) #6 Making connections between visual arts and other disciplines

① Teach

Ask children to make a large circle with their arms, a medium-sized circle with their fingertips, and a small circle with their thumb and index finger.

Display page 22 and read the page aloud. Talk about ideas expressed in the artwork. For instance, say: **This artwork has different shapes of different sizes. The shapes are organized together to create a nice artwork.** Give children time to discuss the artwork. Have them describe the big and small shapes. (big leaf shapes, small circles) Help children see that some shapes have straight edges while others have curved edges. Ask:

- **What do the shapes remind you of?** (leaves, berries, hearts, a window looking out)

Lesson 3

Shape

Artists show **shapes** in their artwork.
Circles, squares, and triangles are shapes.
Find some big and small shapes.

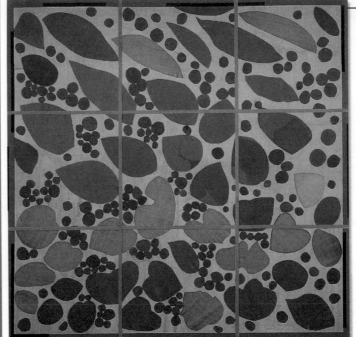

Henri Matisse. *Ivy in Flower*, 1953. Colored paper and pencil, 112 by 112 inches. Dallas Museum of Art, Foundation for the Arts Collection, gift of the Albert and Mary Lasker Foundation.

22

 Art Background

Ivy in Flower Henri Matisse (1869–1954) created this large artwork about a year before he died. Confined to his bed during this period of his life, he was unable to paint and so he turned to drawing and then to cut-paper artworks called collages. Sometimes he spent days arranging and rearranging the shapes in an artwork.

 Notes

To help children learn the names of shapes, put different-size circles, squares, and triangles in a bag. Children can take turns pulling a shape out of the bag, tracing along its outer edge, and saying its name after you: **This is a (square).**

Paste Shapes

Studio 3

1. **Pick.**
2. **Paste.**
3. **Press.**
4. **Repeat.**

Think Like an Artist

Which shapes did you use? Why?

 Curriculum Connection

Math Show children how to use a ruler to make straight lines. Let them experiment with connecting points and lines to create shapes with straight edges. They can copy some of their shapes in their Sketchbook Journals.

 Meeting Individual Needs

Extend To engage children who typically finish quickly, suggest that they sort their shapes first before they arrange them on their paper and paste them down. Encourage them to explain how they sorted the shapes, such as by size, color, or shape.

② Create

Invite children to look at the pictures as you point to and read the steps on page 23.

Before children begin, point out that once they paste a shape on the paper, it is hard to move it. Ask them to arrange some or all of their shapes before they begin pasting.

Technique Tip Tell children that the paste always goes on the smaller piece along the edge, *not* on the large sheet of paper. Remind them to use as little paste as possible.

Quick Studio Have children experiment with different shapes in their Sketchbook Journals. They can use pencils, markers, or crayons to draw shapes.

③ Close

Have children use the *Think Like an Artist* questions to express ideas about their own work. (I used squares and triangles, but no circles; Squares and triangles are my favorite shapes.)

Ongoing Assessment

If . . . children have trouble with sticky fingers,

then . . . suggest that they use less paste and wipe their fingers on a damp paper towel.

See page 18 from **Unit-by-Unit Resources** for a rubric to assess this studio.

Look and Compare

Look and Compare

At a Glance

Objectives

- Compare and contrast two artworks about the same subject.
- Respond to and make judgments about artworks.

Materials

- **Art Prints 1, 2, 3**

NVAS (K–4) #5 Reflecting upon and assessing the characteristics and merits of their work and the work of others

Explore

Display **Art Print 1,** *Hare*. Help children recall this watercolor by Albrecht Dürer from page 16. As children look at the two artworks on pages 24 and 25, invite them to predict which one was also created by Dürer, and give reasons for their answer. (*Screech Owl* because the owl has a lot of tiny lines in it, like the painting of the hare.)

Ask children to share their ideas about the two paintings by Dürer. Model by saying: **Both of these artworks are realistic. I want to touch them because they look as if they are soft.**

Discuss

Read aloud pages 24 and 25. Have children identify the subject of each artwork. (owl, frog) Invite them to look at the light and curved lines used in Dürer's watercolor. Explain that these light and curved lines in this painting help make the feathers, eyes, and talons look more realistic. Children can contrast this with the bold, thick lines of Parsons's artwork.

Animals in Art

Many artists like to show animals in their artwork. Which animal looks almost real?

Albrecht Dürer. *Screech Owl*, 1508. Watercolor, pen, and brush on paper, 7½ by 5½ inches. Graphische Sammlung Albertina, Vienna, Austria.

24

 **Art Background**

Screech Owl Albrecht Dürer was a great observer of his surroundings. This watercolor is one of several in which he sought to capture the beauty of nature. With shades of just brown, white, and black, Dürer captured the essence of an owl—its alert and watchful gaze, its sharp talons seemingly ready to pounce, its downy feathers.

Winged Frog Betty Parsons (1900–1982) was an artist and a gallery owner in New York. In her whimsical sculptures made from found objects, she experimented with form and texture.

What is the same about these artworks?

What is different?

Betty Parsons. (American, 1900–1982). *Winged Frog*, 1978. Mixed-media wood construction, 27 by 20 inches. The National Museum of Women in the Arts, Washington, D.C., gift of Wallace and Wilhelmina Holladay.

25

 Reading Strategy

Use Graphic Organizers Display a simple graphic organizer that children use often, such as a chart showing classroom jobs or a daily schedule. Read the chart, then show children how the chart is arranged so that you can find information quickly, such as who passes out snacks or what time everyone goes to lunch.

Apply

Draw a Venn diagram like the one below on the chalkboard. Tell children that this graphic organizer is a good way to show how two artworks are the same and different.

To fill in the diagram, suggest that children first compare the artworks, looking for ways they are alike. Fill in the middle section as children suggest ideas.

Guide children as they look for differences by suggesting that they focus on the lines and shapes in the two artworks. Tell them to be respectful of differing opinions as they share ideas about the artworks. Possible responses are shown in blue.

Animal Artwork

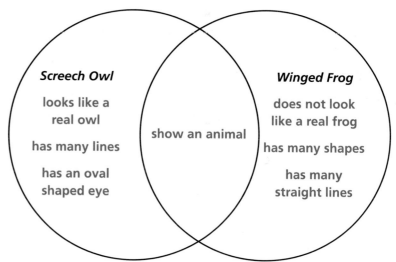

Screech Owl

looks like a real owl

has many lines

has an oval shaped eye

show an animal

Winged Frog

does not look like a real frog

has many shapes

has many straight lines

Close

Ask children what they learned about animals from these two artists. (Possible response: that each animal has its own shape and body parts)

Lesson 4

At a Glance

Objectives

- Identify and describe the five senses.
- Use a magazine picture to make an artwork.
- Respond to and make judgments about artworks.

Materials

- old magazines, scissors ⚠, glue, crayons, construction paper, trays
- Rubric 1 from **Unit-by-Unit Resources**

Vocabulary

senses

NVAS (K–4) #1 Understanding and applying media, techniques, and processes

NVAS (K–4) #2 Using knowledge of structures and functions

NVAS (K–4) #3 Choosing and evaluating a range of subject matter, symbols, and ideas

NVAS (K–4) #6 Making connections between visual arts and other disciplines

① Teach

Teach children a chant about their senses. For example, touch your eyes as you say: **I can see, see, see/With my eyes, eyes, eyes.** Continue with the other senses and sense organs: **I can hear, hear, hear/With my ears, ears, ears,** and so on. Give examples of different objects that children can see, hear, taste, smell, or touch.

Display page 26 and discuss the painting. Mention that as you look at the painting, you can imagine being in the kitchen, hearing people talk, and smelling the *empanadas,* little pies with fruit or meat inside. Then ask:

- **Where do you see circles and half-circles in the painting?** (the plates, the bowls, the *empanadas*)
- **How do you think one of these *empanadas* would taste?** (sweet if it has fruit, spicy if it has meat)

Lesson 4

Senses

Artists use their **senses** to plan artworks.

They see, hear, smell, touch, and taste.

What could you taste in this painting?

Carmen Lomas Garza. *Empanadas,* 1991. Gouache painting, 20 by 28 inches. © 1991 Carmen Lomas Garza. Collection of Romeo Montalvo, M.D., Brownsville, TX. Photograph by Judy Reed.

26

 Art Background

Art and Culture Carmen Lomas Garza (1948–) has painted many scenes from her childhood in Kingsville, Texas. By showing everyday events in her Mexican American home and community, she hopes people from different backgrounds will see how her family's traditions are similar to their own.

ESL Notes

Model touching your mouth as you say: **This is my mouth.** Encourage children to mimic you. Then pantomime eating and drinking and have them join in. Ask: **Do I hear or taste with my mouth?** Continue with other sense organs.

Use Your Senses

1 **Choose.**

2 **Paste.**

3 **Press.**

4 **Draw.**

Think Like an Artist

Which senses does your picture show?

27

 Technology

Make a Poster Give children access to a simple clip art program. Invite them to make a poster that shows something they like to feel, see, hear, smell, or touch. They can choose clip art to illustrate their poster and write a label for their picture, such as **I like to smell flowers.**

 Meeting Individual Needs

Inclusion Provide textured paper and fabric for children who are visually impaired to touch and add to their senses collage.

2 Create

Invite children to look at the pictures as you point to and read the steps. Prior to the activity, gather some magazine pictures. Have children choose one picture that they would like to use in their artwork.

In Step 4, model for children how to use crayons or markers to draw lines around the sensory image they chose.

Technique Tip In Step 4, children can either draw a scene that includes the object they selected, or they can add lines and shapes to make a frame or design around the object.

Quick Studio Have children draw something they like to taste or smell. As they share their drawings, classmates can guess the food, flower, or other object.

3 Close

Have children use the *Think Like an Artist* question to express ideas about their own work. (Possible response: My picture of popcorn shows something I can see, hear, and touch.)

Ongoing Assessment

If . . . children have trouble making a variety of lines around their cutout,

then . . . review kinds of lines by drawing them in the air.

See page 18 from **Unit-by-Unit Resources** for a rubric to assess this studio.

Lesson 5

Lesson 5

At a Glance

Objectives

- Identify and describe colors.
- Use crayons to make an original arkwork.
- Respond to and make judgments about artworks.

Materials

- bag, objects that are one color, crayons, white drawing paper
- Rubric 1 from **Unit-by-Unit Resources**

Vocabulary

colors

NVAS (K–4) #1 Understanding and applying media, techniques, and processes

NVAS (K–4) #2 Using knowledge of structures and functions

NVAS (K–4) #3 Choosing and evaluating a range of subject matter, symbols, and ideas

NVAS (K–4) #6 Making connections between visual arts and other disciplines

Color

There are **colors** all around you.

Artists use many different colors.

Name the colors in the painting.

Marc Chagall. *Green Violinist,* 1923–1924. Oil on canvas, 78 by 42¾ inches. Solomon R. Guggenheim Museum, New York.

28

① Teach

Teach children a song about colors. As everyone sings a verse, children wearing that color can stand up and point to the color on his or her clothing. Substitute color words in this version of "Hot Cross Buns": **Green, green, green/Green, green, green/I see green/You see green/Green, green, green.**

Display page 28 and describe the painting. Talk about the artist's use of color. Ask:

- **What is unusual about the violinist's face?** (It is green.)
- **Why do you think the artist used colors the way he did?** (to get our attention, to show how he feels about music)

 Art Background

Green Violinist This painting, by Marc Chagall (1887–1985), was painted after the artist moved to Paris from Russia. Like many of Chagall's artworks, it shows his love and nostalgia for the village of his childhood, where music and dance were so important in people's lives.

 Notes

Give each child a few crayons of different colors. Model asking a question: **Ana, do you have red?** The child can respond by nodding, by saying yes or no, or by answering the question: **Yes, I have red.** Encourage children to ask each other color questions too.

Draw with Colors

1 **Choose.**

2 **Find.**

3 **Draw.**

4 **Repeat.**

Think Like an Artist

Which color is your favorite? Why?

29

 Fine Arts Connection

Music Talk about fiddles and other stringed instruments. Have children make their own by stretching rubber bands across empty margarine tubs and then plucking the "strings." Invite children to play their instrument while singing familiar songs.

 Meeting Individual Needs

Extend Invite children to name objects that have two colors. They can draw what they see and then add the two colors with markers or crayons.

2 Create

In advance, collect items that are a single color, such as a green leaf, a blue ribbon, a brown button, an orange, and so on. Place the objects in one or more bags.

Have children look at the pictures as you point to and read the steps. Explain that in Step 1, each child chooses a colored object from a bag. That will be the color crayon he or she starts drawing with. Children will continue choosing other objects to know what colors to add to their drawing.

Technique Tip Encourage children to experiment with color. Model, for example, how to make light and dark hues using the same crayon.

Quick Studio Display fruits or vegetables. Have children choose one to draw and color.

3 Close

Have children use the *Think Like an Artist* questions to reflect on their own work. (My favorite color is red. It is bright and it makes me happy.)

Ongoing Assessment

If . . . children have trouble deciding what to draw with a certain color,

then . . . show them Chagall's painting as an example of how artists use colors in surprising ways.

See page 18 from **Unit-by-Unit Resources** for a rubric to assess this studio.

Lesson 6

At a Glance

Objectives

- Identify and describe warm and cool colors.
- Use crayons to draw yourself feeling a certain way.
- Respond to and make judgments about artworks.

Materials

- crayons, white drawing paper
- Rubric 1 from **Unit-by-Unit Resources**

Vocabulary

warm colors, cool colors

NVAS (K–4) #1 Understanding and applying media, techniques, and processes

NVAS (K–4) #2 Using knowledge of structures and functions

NVAS (K–4) #3 Choosing and evaluating a range of subject matter, symbols, and ideas

NVAS (K–4) #6 Making connections between visual arts and other disciplines

① Teach

Tell children that colors are divided into groups. Ask: **Which colors are bright and cheerful?** Lead children to say yellow, red, and orange. Hold up the appropriate crayons as you explain that they are called *warm colors.*

Then ask: **What colors are cool and calm?** Lead children to say blue, green, and violet. Hold up these crayons as you tell them that these colors are called *cool colors.*

Display page 30 and read the page aloud. Ask children to express ideas about Picasso's painting. Ask:

- **Why do you think the artist used cool colors instead of warm colors?** (Possible responses: to help us feel the sadness or love that the girl is feeling)

Warm and Cool Colors

Red, orange, and yellow are **warm colors.**

Green, blue, and violet are **cool colors.**

Artists use these colors to show feelings.

Pablo Picasso. *Child with a Dove,* 1901. Oil on canvas, 29½ by 21⅜ inches. Private collection, London. Photograph © AKG London. © 1998 Estate of Pablo Picasso/Artists Rights Society (ARS), New York.

 Art Background

About the Artist Pablo Picasso (1881–1973) is generally regarded as the most important artist of the twentieth century. Highly prolific and innovative in painting, sculpture, and collage, he has influenced artists and styles of art around the world.

 Notes

Sing and clap the song "If You're Happy and You Know It, Clap Your Hands." Encourage children to join in however they can. Stamp your feet for *angry* and pretend to cry for *sad.* Exaggerate your facial expressions as you sing about different feelings.

Color Feelings

1 Think.

2 Choose.

3 Draw.

4 Color.

Think Like an Artist

What colors show how you feel?

31

Curriculum Connection

Social Studies Invite children to role-play classroom situations that can cause strong feelings, such as not sharing materials. Remind children to tell each other how they are feeling and why: *I am angry because you won't share the crayons.*

Meeting Individual Needs

Reteach When drawing themselves, most five-year-olds tend to show just the parts that they consider important. A drawing that seems incomplete to you may be perfectly acceptable to the artist. Invite the child to tell you about it privately.

2 Create

Ask children to look at the pictures as you point to and read the steps on page 31. In Step 1, help children brainstorm objects, people, or places that make them happy (or sad). Then they can choose warm or cool colors to convey how they are feeling in their picture. Point out that they may want to add something that is special to them, like the dove the girl is holding in the painting.

Technique Tip Have children use their entire paper to draw themselves. Point out that they may want to leave room for a special object.

Quick Studio Set up a table with only cool colors and a table with only warm colors. Children can identify the colors and then choose which place to complete their drawing.

3 Close

Have children use the *Think Like an Artist* question to express ideas about their own work. (Possible responses: I used yellow to show that I am happy.)

Ongoing Assessment

If . . . children have trouble adding details,

then . . . have a classmate describe some details to add.

See page 18 from **Unit-by-Unit Resources** for a rubric to assess this studio.

At a Glance

Objectives

- Read about a career in art.
- Relate art to personal experiences.

Materials

- picture books
- Sketchbook Journals

Vocabulary

illustrations

NVAS (K–4) #5 Reflecting upon and assessing the characteristics and merits of their work and the work of others

NVAS (K–4) #6 Making connections between visual arts and other disciplines

Explore

Display a variety of picture books that children are familiar with, including one by Lois Ehlert if possible, such as *Color Zoo* or *Eating the Alphabet*. Page through the books and tell how the pictures help a reader understand the story.

Discuss

Read aloud pages 32 and 33. Help children relate the job of picture-book illustrator to their everyday life. Ask: **Where can you find artwork by this artist?** (in my picture books) Then ask children to express ideas about Ehlert's illustrations on page 33.

Explain that other book illustrators might use different tools, such as paintbrushes and paint, a camera, or chalk to make their pictures, because each artist has a unique style.

- **Look at the photograph of the artist at work. What art tools is she using?** (scissors, paper)
- **When you write a story, which part do you like—writing the words or drawing the pictures? Why?** (Answers will vary.)

Picture Books

Lois Ehlert makes books for children. She writes the stories and creates the **illustrations,** or pictures.

Lois Ehlert

32

 Career Research

Have children go to the library to look for other kinds of art in picture books. Invite them to find at least one book with illustrations that are photographs. To help children understand how a particular book's illustrations were made, refer to the book jacket, which often gives information about the illustration process. Many children's book illustrators, including Lois Ehlert, can also be researched on the World Wide Web.

Ehlert wrote the book, *Color Zoo*.

What lines, shapes, and colors did she use?

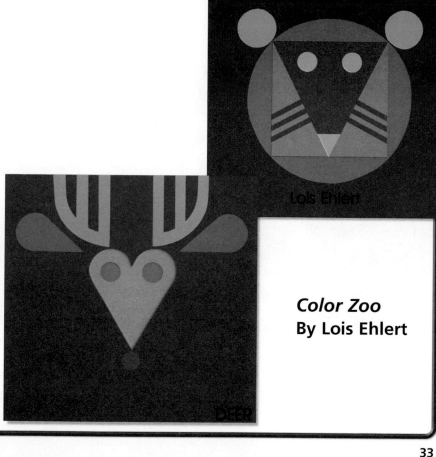

Color Zoo
By Lois Ehlert

33

Apply

Ask children to watch as you create a graphic organizer like the one below. Tell them they will help you fill in the empty boxes to tell about the art in picture books. For the first column, invite children to suggest kinds of illustrations. In the second column, write the art tools that are needed. Possible responses are shown below.

Kinds of Illustrations	Art Tools
paintings	paintbrushes, paints
photographs	camera
cut paper	scissors, paper, glue

Close

Review the completed graphic organizer and ask: **If you were a book illustrator, what type of pictures would you like to create?** (I would paint my pictures, because I enjoy painting the most.)

Sketchbook Journal Children can draw ideas for their own illustrated storybooks.

 Reading Strategy

Use Prior Knowledge Tell children that they can use what they already know about picture books to understand Ehlert's job. Remind them that every time they read or listen to a story, they use the illustrations to understand what is happening. Invite volunteers to share their own illustrated stories, telling about the art tools they used and how they decided what to show in each picture. Relate this prior knowledge to Ehlert's career.

Portfolio Project

Portfolio Project

At a Glance

Objectives

- Develop and organize ideas from the environment.
- Demonstrate knowledge about line, shape, and color.
- Evaluate original artworks by self and peers.

Materials

- Sketchbook Journals
- crayons or markers, scissors ⚠, colored construction paper, large drawing paper, paste or glue
- Rubric 1 from **Unit-by-Unit Resources**

NVAS (K–4) #1 Understanding and applying media, techniques, and processes

NVAS (K–4) #5 Reflecting upon and assessing the characteristics and merits of their work and the work of others

Draw Yourself

❶ Draw.

❷ Cut.

❸ Paste.

❹ Color.

34

Plan

Tell children they will be making *self-portraits*, or pictures of themselves. Encourage other children to tell how they will use line, shape, and color to show other body parts, clothing, and shoes.

Ask:

- **What shape will you draw for your head?**
- **What color will you make your shirt?**
- **Will you make yourself big or small on the paper? Why?**

Quick Project

Have children draw themselves. Provide precut shapes for children to add clothing.

🚶‍♂️🚶‍♀️ Meeting Individual Needs

Reteach To help children complete Step 2 successfully, model how to choose a sheet of colored construction paper and draw a simple item of clothing. Point out how you make it the right size, so that it will fit the figure that the child has drawn. If children have difficulty with using scissors, offer to cut around the "tricky" parts, letting them cut the straight and curved lines.

Look at these self-portraits.

What shapes did the children use?

Abbie, Age 5. *Abbie and Flowers*. Crayon and construction paper.

John Allen, Age 5. *Big Muscles*. Crayon and construction paper.

Share Your Art

1. Name the shapes you used.

2. Describe one problem you had.

35

 Gallery Options

Classroom Portrait Gallery After children have had a chance to show and tell about their self-portraits, create a display in which each portrait is shown next to a recent photograph of that child. Children can write a label to display next to their artwork. You may wish to talk about credit lines and the information they contain—the name of the artist, the name of the artwork, the date when it was finished, and the media used (for example, crayons and cut paper).

Create

Read page 34 and model each step. Then guide children to complete the project:

- Remind them to use most of the paper so that their self-portrait will be easy to see.
- If children have difficulty cutting out their clothing items, suggest that they cut a circle around the shape they drew. They can ask a classmate or teacher to cut closer to the lines.
- Remind children to put the paste on the edges of the item being pasted instead of on the white drawing paper.
- Point out interesting lines, shapes, and colors children are using to add details. For example: **Maya is drawing zigzag lines on her shirt.**

If you plan to have children display their artworks using the suggestion in *Gallery Options,* provide a large space where you can store the self-portraits.

Close

Point out the children's art on page 35. Explain that these artworks are from the portfolios of other kindergartners. Ask:

- **What shapes do you see in these artworks?** (rectangles, circles, triangles)
- **What do you like about these artworks?** (Possible response: I like how they used squares and rectangles to make clothes.)

Use the prompts in *Share Your Art* to help children express ideas about their own artwork. (I used squares, triangles, and circles. I had trouble lining up the clothes I made to my head.)

See page 18 from **Unit-by-Unit Resources** for a rubric to assess this project.

Unit 1 Review

At a Glance

Objectives

- Relate art terms to the environment.
- Identify line, shape, and color in artworks.
- Describe, analyze, interpret, and judge an artwork.

Materials

- **Art Print 4**
- children's art portfolios

NVAS (K–4) **#1** Understanding and applying media, techniques, and processes

NVAS (K–4) **#2** Using knowledge of structures and functions

NVAS (K–4) **#5** Reflecting upon and assessing the characteristics and merits of their work and the work of others

Think About Art

Possible responses include:

line (Point to lines.)
shape (Point to shapes.)
drawing (Point to the cow.)
artist (Point to artist.)

Talk About Art

Help children look through their portfolio for an artwork they want to share. As children share their artwork, encourage them to use words such as *line, shape,* and *color* to express ideas about what they did.

 Think About Art

Find a picture for each word.

line   shape   artist   drawing

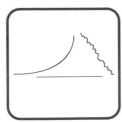 

 Talk About Art

- Look through your portfolio.
- Choose an artwork you like.
- Tell why you like it.

36

 Assessment Options

Options for assessing children appear in the **Unit-by-Unit Resources.**

- Use the **Vocabulary Worksheets** on pages 11–14 for an informal assessment of Unit 1 vocabulary.
- Use the **Unit 1 Test** on pages 19–22 to assess children's mastery of unit vocabulary and concepts.

Joan Miró. *Illustration for the book,*
Talking Alone, 1948. Smithsonian
American Art Museum, Washington, D.C.

Put It All Together

1. What colors do you see?

2. Which shapes are smallest?

3. What does it remind you of?

4. Where would you hang this painting? Why?

37

Put It All Together

Use the questions on page 37 to express ideas about the artwork. Possible responses follow.

1. The artist used black, red, yellow, green, purple, and blue. DESCRIBE

2. The smallest shapes are the circles that look like fingertips. ANALYZE

3. Pictures that my friends draw of themselves INTERPRET

4. Children might say they would hang the picture in their classroom to add bright colors and interesting shapes. JUDGE

 Art Background

About the Artist Joan Miró (1893–1983) was a Spanish Surrealist artist. Surrealism is a twentieth-century movement in art that emphasizes the expression of the subconscious through fantastic imagery. For a short time in his career, Miró painted realistic still lifes and portraits. But soon, he came to admire the freedom that more abstract painting allowed. Eventually, he found his style in his childlike and dreamy paintings that use bright colors, rich blacks, and organic forms.

Unit 2 Overview

Art can be found in the nearby environment. It can be explored through the five senses. In this unit, children will learn about the people who use paints and paintbrushes to create art. They will use their senses to discover art and create their own artworks using the elements of art and principles of design.

	Unit Opener, p. 38	Lesson 1, p. 40 **Texture** **Studio 1, p. 41** Make a Texture Collage	Lesson 2, p. 42 **Paintings** **Studio 2, p. 43** Paint a Picture	Lesson 3, p. 44 **Colors Together** **Studio 3, p. 45** Mix Two Colors	Look and Compare, p. 46 **Children in Paintings**
Artworks	**Pablo Picasso.** *Le Gourmet,* 1901.		**Gabriele Münter.** *Child with Ball,* ca. 1916.	**Helen Frankenthaler.** *Small's Paradise,* 1964.	**Pablo Picasso.** *Paul Dressed as a Harlequin,* 1924. **Francisco Goya.** *Don Manuel Osorio Manrrique de Zuñiga,* ca. 1784.
Vocabulary		texture	paintbrush		
Materials	• **Art Print 5** • **Instructional Prints**	• flat, textured objects, such as fabric scraps, buttons, leaves; construction paper; glue; trays	• paintbrushes, tempera paints, jars of water, muffin tins, paper towels, paint smocks	• transparent color paddles (optional) • paintbrushes, tempera paints, jars of water, muffin tins, paper towels, paint smocks • paint palettes (optional)	**Art Prints 5, 6, 7**
Connections	**Home Connection** Art in the home, neighborhood, or community **Bookshelf** *Picasso for Kids (The Great Art for Kids Series)* by Margaret E. Hyde, Budding Artists, Inc., 1996	**Visual Culture** textures at home **ESL Notes** **Fine Arts Connection** Music: sound textures **Meeting Individual Needs** Inclusion	**Technology** Paint pictures **ESL Notes** **Meeting Individual Needs** Inclusion	**ESL Notes** **Curriculum Connection** Health: colorful foods **Meeting Individual Needs** Extend	**Reading Strategy** Set a purpose
Assessment Opportunities		Rubric 2 from **Unit-by-Unit Resources** Ongoing Assessment	Rubric 2 from **Unit-by-Unit Resources** Ongoing Assessment	Rubric 2 from **Unit-by-Unit Resources** Ongoing Assessment	

Lesson 4, p. 48 More Colors Studio 4, p. 49 Mix More Colors	Lesson 5, p. 50 Pattern Studio 5, p. 51 Make a Rubbing	Lesson 6, p. 52 Family Pictures Studio 6, p. 53 Draw a Family	Artist at Work, p. 54 Kaleidoscopes	Portfolio Project, p. 56 Paint Animals with Texture	Unit Review, p. 58
Franz Marc. *The Large Blue Horses,* 1911.	**Sisson Blanchard.** *Chickens (Volailles),* ca. 1965.	**Artist unknown.** *Cat and Kittens,* ca. 1872–1883.	A kaleidoscope by Carolyn Bennett		**Edward Hicks.** *The Peaceable Kingdom,* ca. 1840–1845.
	pattern	subject			
• six sheets of colored construction paper • muffin tins; paintbrushes; red, blue, and yellow tempera paints; jars of water; damp paper towels; paint smocks; paper plates; white drawing paper; color chips (optional)	• clothing catalog or magazine • crayons without wrappers; newsprint; flat textured objects such as fabric, leaves, mesh screens, etc.	• drawing paper; wrapped and unwrapped crayons; flat, textured objects for crayon rubbings	• kaleidoscopes • Sketchbook Journals	• small plastic models of animals (optional) • muffin tins of red, blue, yellow, orange, violet, and green paint; paintbrushes; drawing paper; newsprint; baby food jars of water; paper towels; scissors ⚠; crayons; flat, textured objects; paste or glue	• **Art Print 8** • children's art portfolios
ESL Notes **Curriculum Connection** Science: make sun catchers **Meeting Individual Needs** Reteach	**ESL Notes** **Curriculum Connection** Math: make patterns **Meeting Individual Needs** Inclusion	**ESL Notes** **Fine Arts Connection** Theatre: role-play a family member **Meeting Individual Needs** Extend	**Career Research** Craftspersons and their hobbies or careers **Reading Strategy** Identify cause and effect relationships	**Gallery Options** Multimedia show **Meeting Individual Needs** Reteach, Extend	
Rubric 2 from **Unit-by-Unit Resources** Ongoing Assessment	Rubric 2 from **Unit-by-Unit Resources** Ongoing Assessment	Rubric 2 from **Unit-by-Unit Resources** Ongoing Assessment		Rubric 2 from **Unit-by-Unit Resources**	**Unit-by-Unit Resources** Vocabulary Worksheets, pp. 29–32 Unit 2 Test, pp. 37–40

Unit 2

Objectives

- Identify elements of art in artworks.
- Relate art to personal experiences.
- Respond to and make judgments about artworks.

Materials

- **Art Print 5**

NVAS (K–4) #4 Understanding the visual arts in relation to history and cultures

NVAS (K–4) #5 Reflecting upon and assessing the characteristics and merits of their work and the work of others

Introduce the Unit

Read the title of Unit 2. Explain to children that in this unit they will learn that they can use all of their senses to discover and enjoy art in their environment. Display *Le Gourmet* and share your ideas about Picasso's painting. Have children join in by sharing their ideas. Remind them to be respectful of people with differing opinions.

Then read the poem, "Little Blue Girl." Reread the poem inviting children to join in. After reading it, ask a volunteer to suggest what the girl's treat might be. Say the poem several times so that children can join in and suggest different treats.

Help children relate the words in the poem to the painting of the girl. Ask:

- **Why do you think the artist used mostly blue paint?** (Possible responses: he liked blue, he wanted to make us feel a certain way)

Pablo Picasso. *Le Gourmet*, 1901. Oil on canvas, 36½ by 26⅞ inches. National Gallery of Art, Washington, D.C.

38

 Art Background

Le Gourmet Pablo Picasso (1881–1973) explored many artistic styles during his life. *Le Gourmet* is a painting from his so-called "Blue Period." Many of the paintings from this period are mostly shades of blue and show a solitary figure standing in silent contemplation.

 Home Connection

Suggest to children that they go with a family member to look for art in their home, neighborhood, or community. Encourage them to take photographs or make sketches of the artworks to share with their classmates.

Art Nearby

Little Blue Girl

Little blue girl,

What do you see?

A treat for you?

What could it be?

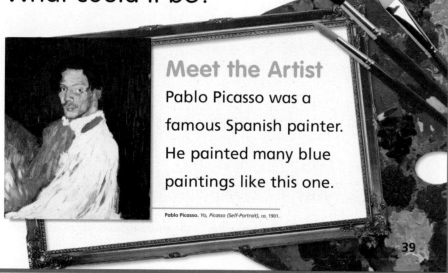

Meet the Artist

Pablo Picasso was a famous Spanish painter. He painted many blue paintings like this one.

Pablo Picasso. *Yo, Picasso (Self-Portrait)*, ca. 1901.

39

 Bookshelf

Picasso for Kids (The Great Art for Kids Series)
by Margaret E. Hyde
Budding Artists, Inc., 1996

This book is one in a series that introduces children to some of the most influential artists of our time, such as Vincent van Gogh, Henri Matisse, and Pablo Picasso.

Discuss Unit Concepts

Point to the self-portrait of Pablo Picasso on page 39 and tell children that the painter who created *Le Gourmet* also painted this picture of himself. After reading the information about Picasso, explain that in this unit, children will learn about artists like Picasso who used paints and paintbrushes to make artworks. Ask children to share any personal experiences they have had with painting. Encourage them to use sensory words to tell about the look, smell, and feel of the paint.

As you introduce each element of art and principle of design in Unit 2, you may wish to display the **Instructional Prints.** A print is provided for each element and principle.

Meet the Artist

Pablo Picasso (1881–1973) Pablo Picasso, the son of an art professor, was recognized at an early age for his artistic ability. When he took the entrance exam at age 14 for the Academy of Fine Arts in Barcelona, Spain, he finished it in one day! Most students took a full month to complete the same assignment. Picasso is credited with being one of the founders of Cubism and one of the first collage artists. He was also an accomplished sculptor.

Lesson 1

Lesson 1

At a Glance

Objectives

- Identify and describe textures in the environment.
- Use textured objects in an artwork.
- Respond to and make judgments about artworks.

Materials

- flat, textured objects, such as fabric scraps, buttons, leaves; construction paper; glue; trays
- Rubric 2 from **Unit-by-Unit Resources**

Vocabulary

texture

NVAS (K–4) #1 Understanding and applying media, techniques, and processes

NVAS (K–4) #2 Using knowledge of structures and functions

NVAS (K–4) #3 Choosing and evaluating a range of subject matter, symbols, and ideas

NVAS (K–4) #6 Making connections between visual arts and other disciplines

Texture

Texture is the way an object feels.

Choose an object.

Tell how it feels.

① Teach

Have volunteers name things they like to touch, such as soft or smooth objects, and things they do not like to touch, such as rough or sharp objects. Explain to children that when they describe how an object feels, they are describing its texture. Then have children imagine they are in the photograph as you read the text aloud. Ask:

- **How would the moss feel if you touched it?** (soft, spongy) **The tree trunk?** (hard, rough)
- **Tell about something else in a forest that would have texture.** (Possible responses: furry animal, hard rocks, bumpy soil, etc.)

 Visual Culture

Ask a volunteer to suggest a room in their home, such as a kitchen or a bathroom. Invite children to think of different textures they would find in that room.

 Notes

Collect a variety of textured objects, such as rough and smooth rocks, hard buttons and soft fabrics. Touch an object, such as a rock and say: **This rock feels smooth.** Invite children to feel the same object and repeat the sentence. Help them describe the textures of other objects.

Make a Texture Collage

1 Touch.

2 Choose.

3 Arrange.

4 Glue.

Art in My World

Name an object in your classroom that is smooth.

41

 Fine Arts Connection

Music Pass out musical instruments. Model for children how they can create different sound textures to "feel" with their ears. (sand blocks sound rough; bells sound soft)

 Meeting Individual Needs

Inclusion Children who are visually impaired usually have a highly developed sense of touch. Encourage them to help others choose and describe textures.

2 Create

Tell children they will use their sense of touch to create an artwork with textures. Have them look at the pictures as you point to and read the steps. Show them some of the objects for gluing, and have them brainstorm how they might arrange them in an artwork.

Before children begin Step 3, model arranging the forms to create different designs.

Technique Tip Remind children to use as little glue as possible, and to wipe up any excess with a damp paper towel.

⏱ **Quick Studio** Let children choose objects to arrange in a textured still life that they can draw.

3 Close

Use the *Art in My World* activity to help children glean information from the environment using their senses.

Ongoing Assessment

If . . . children find that their objects are falling off,

then . . . have them reapply the glue and hold the object down as they count to ten.

See page 36 from **Unit-by-Unit Resources** for a rubric to assess this studio.

Lesson 2

At a Glance

Objectives

- Identify and explore painting.
- Use paint and a paintbrush to make an original artwork.
- Respond to and make judgments about artworks.

Materials

- paintbrushes, tempera paints, jars of water, muffin tins, paper towels, paint smocks
- Rubric 2 from **Unit-by-Unit Resources**

Vocabulary

paintbrush

NVAS (K–4) #1 Understanding and applying media, techniques, and processes

NVAS (K–4) #2 Using knowledge of structures and functions

NVAS (K–4) #3 Choosing and evaluating a range of subject matter, symbols, and ideas

1 Teach

Hold a paintbrush in front of you as if you are painting a picture. Tell children to imagine they have a paintbrush too. As you lead them in "painting" long lines, small dots, and other marks, tell children they are painting a painting.

Display and read aloud page 42. Have children discuss the painting. Model by saying: **I can see the brush strokes in the painting. It looks different than a drawing.** Ask children to continue by expressing their ideas about Münter's painting. Ask:

- **Where do you see textures that the artist made with the paintbrush?** (Possible responses: in her furry hat and soft skin)

As children tell a story about the painting, they might say that the girl is dressed to go outside and play with her ball.

42

Lesson 2

Paintings

Some artworks are made with paint and a **paintbrush.** Tell a story about this painting.

Gabriele Münter. *Child with Ball*, ca. 1916. Oil on canvas, 20½ x 17 inches. The National Museum of Women in the Arts, Washington, D.C. On loan from the Wallace and Wilhelmina Holladay Collection. © 1998 Artists Rights Society (ARS), New York/VG Bild-Kunst, Bonn.

42

 Art Background

Art and Culture Gabriele Münter (1877–1962) exhibited her work with the German Expressionist group Der Blaue Reiter (The Blue Rider). Expressionists wanted to represent subjective experiences and emotions in their work. This art style flowered in Germany during the early twentieth century.

 Notes

Give each child a paintbrush. Model painting as you say: **I am painting. I hold my paintbrush like this. I can make a tall line.** Encourage children to repeat your sentences as they follow along with their paintbrush. Be sure they are holding it correctly.

Paint a Picture

1 Dip.

2 Paint.

3 Wash.

4 Blot.

Think Like an Artist

What kind of lines did you paint?

43

2 Create

Explain to children that they will experiment with paintbrushes to make lines and textures.

Invite children to look at the pictures as you point to and read the steps. Before passing out materials, model for children how to hold a paintbrush correctly and how to press it gently on the paper.

Technique Tip Some children may tend to "scrub" with their brush instead of paint. Tell them not to press as hard and to dip the brush in the paint whenever it starts to get too dry.

Quick Studio Have children use one color to practice making lines and textures.

3 Close

Have children use the *Think Like an Artist* question to express ideas about their own work. (Possible response: I made thick lines and some that were feathery.)

Ongoing Assessment

If . . . children forget to clean their brush before using a new color,

then . . . point out how muddy the colors become.

See page 36 from **Unit-by-Unit Resources** for a rubric to assess this studio.

 Technology

Paint Pictures Introduce children to the painting tools in a graphics program. Show them how to select the paintbrush and other tools from the tool panel, and how to select colors. Remind them to help each other solve problems as they "paint" a picture on the computer.

 Meeting Individual Needs

Inclusion For children who are unable to hold a paintbrush, adaptive devices are available from medical supply stores.

Lesson 3

At a Glance

Objectives

- Identify and discuss primary colors.
- Use paint to mix colors.
- Respond to and make judgments about artworks.

Materials

- transparent color paddles (optional)
- paintbrushes, tempera paints, jars of water, muffin tins, paper towels, paint smocks
- paint palettes (optional)
- Rubric 2 from **Unit-by-Unit Resources**

NVAS (K–4) #1 Understanding and applying media, techniques, and processes

NVAS (K–4) #2 Using knowledge of structures and functions

NVAS (K–4) #3 Choosing and evaluating a range of subject matter, symbols, and ideas

NVAS (K–4) #6 Making connections between visual arts and other disciplines

1 Teach

Review color names. Have children point to colors in the room or on their clothing. Tell children that red, yellow, and blue are primary colors. If color paddles are available, show children how secondary colors (green, orange, and violet) are made from the three primary colors.

Display page 44 and invite children's ideas about the painting. Ask:

- **The artist mixed blue and yellow in this painting. What color did she make?** (green)

Colors Together

Find orange and green in this painting.

The artist mixed two colors together.

She made new colors.

Helen Frankenthaler. *Small's Paradise*, 1964. Acrylic on canvas, 100 by 93⅝ inches. Smithsonian American Art Museum, Washington, D.C.

44

 Art Background

About the Artist American artist Helen Frankenthaler (1928–) invented the soak-stain technique. Thin washes of color soak into and saturate untreated canvas, providing for a new expression with paint. Frankenthaler herself said, "I am an artist of paint, making discoveries."

 Notes

Hold several crayons. Sing this version of "The Muffin Man" and help children sing their answer as they point to the crayon you name: **Do you see the red crayon? the red crayon? the red crayon?/ Do you see the red crayon that I'm holding in my hand?/ Yes, I see the red crayon, the red crayon, the red crayon, Yes, I see the red crayon that you're holding in your hand.**

Mix Two Colors

1. Dip.
2. Mix.
3. Paint.
4. Wash and blot.

Think Like an Artist

What happens when you mix yellow and red?

45

 Curriculum Connection

Health Tell children that some of the healthiest foods are also the most colorful. Explain to children that foods are called healthy because they help you grow. Invite them to cut out pictures of fruits and vegetables from old food magazines, or draw and color some themselves. Invite volunteers to name their favorite fruit or vegetable.

 Meeting Individual Needs

Extend Pour some white paint in one of the empty muffin tins. Children can experiment with making tints, or lighter hues, by adding a color to the white and mixing well.

2 Create

In advance, pour yellow tempera paint in two sections of each muffin tin. One of the sections should contain less yellow, so that children can mix in some red to make orange. Put red paint in a third section.

Explain to children that they will mix two primary colors to make a new color. Invite them to look at the pictures as you point to and read the steps. Ask volunteers to tell how they will make orange paint.

Technique Tip As children mix red into the yellow to make orange, caution them to add just a little red at a time, since it is the darker color.

Quick Studio Instead of using paints, children can use eyedroppers to drop red- and yellow-colored water onto paper towels. They will see orange where the colors run together.

3 Close

Have children use the *Think Like an Artist* question to reflect on their own work. (It turns into orange.)

Ongoing Assessment

If . . . children mix too much red into the yellow,

then . . . let them start over with fresh yellow and very small amounts of red.

See page 36 from **Unit-by-Unit Resources** for a rubric to assess this studio.

Look and Compare

Look and Compare

At a Glance

Objectives

- Compare and contrast two artworks.
- Respond to and make judgments about artworks.

Materials

- Art Prints 5, 6, 7

NVAS (K–4) #4 Understanding the visual arts in relation to history and cultures

NVAS (K–4) #5 Reflecting upon and assessing the characteristics and merits of their work and the work of others

Explore

Display **Art Print 5,** *Le Gourmet.* Help children recall this painting by Pablo Picasso from page 38. As children look at the two artworks on pages 46 and 47, invite them to predict which one was also created by Picasso. Help children identify that all three artworks have the same simple subject. (a child) Suggest that they look for similar features, such as lines, textures, and colors, to find the second artwork by Picasso. Have them give reasons for their answer. (Possible responses: *Paul Dressed as a Harlequin*; The artist uses blue.)

Discuss

Read aloud pages 46 and 47. To help children find textures, suggest that they focus on lines and colors each artist used. Direct their attention to how Picasso used smudges of color that suggest a soft, velvety fabric on the chair.

Children can compare this to the rich textures in the Goya painting. Children may say the boy is feeling serious, tired, or sad.

Children in Paintings

Pablo Picasso. *Paul Dressed as a Harlequin,* 1924. Oil on canvas, 51½ by 38⅓ inches. Musée Picasso, Paris. Giraudon/Art Resource, NY. © 1998 Estate of Pablo Picasso/Artists Rights Society (ARS), New York.

Find textures in this painting.

How do you think the boy is feeling?

46

 Art Background

Paul Dressed as a Harlequin This painting shows Picasso's eldest son, Paul, at the age of three, dressed in a harlequin costume. Part of the artist's original drawing, which shows another pose, is visible in the lower part of the painting. The bold lines in the costume are offset by the soft, round lines of the boy's face and hands. Picasso kept this painting in his personal collection.

Don Manuel Osorio Manrique de Zuñiga Francisco Goya's affection for children shines through in this portrait. Not quite three, the son of Count Altamira pauses in his play with his pet bird, while his fat hungry cats watch from the shadows. Look for Goya's signature on the card in the bird's beak.

Francisco de Goya. *Don Manuel Osorio Manrrique de Zuniga*, ca. 1784. Oil on canvas, 50 by 40 inches. The Metropolitan Museum of Art, The Jules Bache Collection, 1949. (49.7.41). Photograph © 1994 The Metropolitan Museum of Art.

What textures do you see?

How are these paintings the same?

47

 Reading Strategy

Set a Purpose Tell children that when they read a story or selection, it helps if they set a purpose first. That way, they can focus on specific details. Explain to children that it helps to set a purpose when looking at an artwork as well. To illustrate this idea, tell children that in one of the artworks on pages 46 and 47, a boy loves animals. Encourage children to look at the artworks to determine which boy it is and why. (Goya's painting shows a boy who loves animals. All of his pets are with him.)

Apply

Draw a Venn Diagram like the one below on the chalkboard. Tell children that this graphic organizer is a good way to show how two artworks are the same and different.

To fill in the diagram, suggest that children first compare the artworks, looking for ways they are alike. Fill in the middle section as children suggest ideas. Guide children as they look for differences by suggesting that they focus on the objects in the two artworks. Possible responses are shown in blue.

Paintings of Two Boys

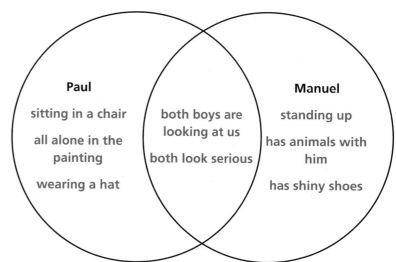

Paul

sitting in a chair

all alone in the painting

wearing a hat

both boys are looking at us

both look serious

Manuel

standing up

has animals with him

has shiny shoes

Close

Ask children to share ideas about how these artists paint children. (Possible responses: each artist has his own way of showing how a child is feeling) Remind children about the importance of demonstrating respect for people with differing opinions.

Lesson 4

At a Glance

Objectives

- Identify and describe primary and secondary colors.
- Use paints to create an original artwork.
- Respond to and make judgments about artworks.

Materials

- six sheets of colored construction paper
- muffin tins; paintbrushes; red, blue, and yellow tempera paints; jars of water; damp paper towels; paint smocks; paper plates; white drawing paper; color chips (optional)
- Rubric 2 from **Unit-by-Unit Resources**

NVAS (K–4) #1 Understanding and applying media, techniques, and processes

NVAS (K–4) #2 Using knowledge of structures and functions

NVAS (K–4) #3 Choosing and evaluating a range of subject matter, symbols, and ideas

NVAS (K–4) #6 Making connections between visual arts and other disciplines

 **Teach**

Have six children stand in front of the group, each holding one sheet of construction paper so that red, blue, yellow, green, orange, and violet are displayed. Ask children holding the red, yellow, and orange colors to stand together to demonstrate how a secondary color is made. Continue, using other primary colors to show how they combine to create secondary colors.

Display page 48 and give children time to describe the colors as well as any other ideas they have about the painting. To answer the second question, children might say that the artist made the horses blue. Ask:

- **What is your favorite part of the painting? Why?** (Answers will vary.)

More Colors

What color are the horses?
How did the artist use color to surprise you?

color wheel

Franz Marc. *The Large Blue Horses*, 1911. Oil on canvas, 43 by 73 inches. Collection Walker Art Center, Minneapolis. Gift of the T.B. Walker Foundation, Gilbert M. Walker Fund, 1942.

48

 Art Background

About the Artist Franz Marc (1880–1916) was a German Expressionist. He is probably best known for his animal motifs, including several paintings of blue horses, in which he sought to show the animals' inner psychology and view of the world.

ESL Notes

Have children practice telling about likes and dislikes as they talk about colors. Help them insert color words in statements such as **I like _____. I don't like _____. My favorite color is _____.**

48

Mix More Colors

1 **Pick.**

2 **Mix.**

3 **Share.**

4 **Paint!**

Think Like an Artist

Tell how you made a new color.

49

 Curriculum Connection

Science Show children how to make sun catchers by gluing colored tissue paper to waxed paper. They can hold their sun catcher in a sunny window to see what bright light does to the colors. Caution children not to look directly at the sun.

 Meeting Individual Needs

Reteach Help children choose partners. Using just two primary colors at a time, partners can mix the colors to make a secondary color. Children can then paint with these three colors, or repeat the mixing process using two other primary colors.

2 Create

Tell children that they will work in teams of three to make paint colors. As you point to and read the steps, remind children about the rules for working in a group.

Explain that in Step 1, each child on a team mixes one color—green, orange, or violet. These paints will be put in the middle of the table so that everyone can use them in Step 4, along with red, yellow, and blue.

Technique Tip In Step 4, give children brushes and paper to use for painting, so that the teams will not run out of their mixed colors too quickly.

Quick Studio Teams can mix secondary colors and then work together to paint a small mural.

3 Close

Have children use the *Think Like an Artist* prompt to reflect on their own work. (Possible response: I mixed red and blue to make violet.)

Ongoing Assessment

If . . . children have trouble working in a group,

then . . . have them work with a partner. See Reteach below.

See page 36 from **Unit-by-Unit Resources** for a rubric to assess this studio.

Lesson 5

Lesson 5

At a Glance

Objectives

- Identify and describe patterns.
- Make a crayon rubbing.
- Respond to and make judgments about artworks.

Materials

- clothing catalog or magazine
- crayons without wrappers; newsprint; flat textured objects such as fabric, leaves, mesh screens, etc.
- Rubric 2 from **Unit-by-Unit Resources**

Vocabulary

pattern

NVAS (K–4) #1 Understanding and applying media, techniques, and processes

NVAS (K–4) #2 Using knowledge of structures and functions

NVAS (K–4) #3 Choosing and evaluating a range of subject matter, symbols, and ideas

NVAS (K–4) #6 Making connections between visual arts and other disciplines

Pattern

This artist used **pattern.**

Some patterns can look like texture.

How do you think the feathers feel?

Sisson Blanchard. *Chickens (Volailles),* ca. 1965. Oil on Masonite panel, 23½ by 48 inches. Collection of Davenport Museum of Art, gift of Dr. Walter E. Neiswanger, M.D. (67.3).

patterns

1 Teach

Display a clothing catalog and talk about how different materials feel. Then invite children to feel their own clothing and describe its texture, such as smooth, soft, bumpy.

Display page 50 and give children time to express ideas about the artwork. As you read the page aloud, explain that patterns are repeated lines, shapes, or colors. To answer the question about visual texture, children may say the feathers would feel soft. Ask:

- **What patterns of lines** (short and curved) **and colors** (black, yellow, red) **are on the feathers?**

Art Background

About the Artist Haitian painter Sisson Blanchard (1929–1981) was a self-taught, or "primitive," artist whose artistic skill was discovered while he was working as a yardman at a Haitian hotel. He did many colorful paintings of barnyard animals and of peasant life in Haiti.

ESL Notes

Invite children to tell about chickens or other birds they have seen. Help them use vocabulary words such as *beak, feathers, wings,* etc. Then have children describe the chickens in the painting, or respond to your directions such as **Touch the black chicken.**

Make a Rubbing

1 Find.

2 Rub.

3 Choose another.

4 Rub.

Think Like an Artist

Tell about the patterns you rubbed.

51

2 Create

Invite each child to choose an object to feel and describe (tactile texture). Then explain that they will follow directions to make the same texture on paper in a rubbing (visual texture).

Invite children to look at the pictures as you point to and read the steps. In Step 2, point out that the child is using the side of a crayon, not the tip. Show them how to make broad strokes across the object after they put it under the paper.

Technique Tip You may wish to model for children what happens when the tip of the crayon is used instead of the side. Using the tip may still produce textures, but often tears the paper.

Quick Studio Partners can take turns choosing the object and the color for the other child to make a rubbing.

3 Close

Have children use the *Think Like an Artist* prompt to reflect on their own work. (Possible response: I rubbed the bumpy pattern on the sandpaper.)

Ongoing Assessment

If . . . children have trouble holding the object still under their paper,

then . . . tape it to the table first.

See page 36 from **Unit-by-Unit Resources** for a rubric to assess this studio.

 Curriculum Connection

Math Have children work with partners. They can take turns making a pattern with counters, blocks, or small toys for the other child to copy. For example, a child might make a line of three different shapes repeated over and over.

 Meeting Individual Needs

Inclusion Children may need help choosing objects that won't cause the paper to tear as they make their rubbing. Green leaves are always a good choice to begin with, because they are soft and very flat, yet have interesting veins and edges.

Lesson 6

At a Glance

Objectives

- Identify and describe the subject of an artwork.
- Draw a family picture and add texture.
- Respond to and make judgments about artworks.

Materials

- drawing paper; wrapped and unwrapped crayons; flat, textured objects for crayon rubbings
- Rubric 2 from **Unit-by-Unit Resources**

Vocabulary

subject

NVAS (K–4) #1 Understanding and applying media, techniques, and processes

NVAS (K–4) #2 Using knowledge of structures and functions

NVAS (K–4) #3 Choosing and evaluating a range of subject matter, symbols, and ideas

NVAS (K–4) #6 Making connections between visual arts and other disciplines

❶ Teach

Teach children this song about families to the tune of "Mary Had a Little Lamb": **Who is in a family, family, family?/ Who is in a family?/ I will tell you now.** Name the people in your family, and then sing the song again several times so that volunteers can tell about a family from a favorite book or television program.

Display page 52 and talk about the cat family. Explain to children that the cat family is the subject of this painting. After you read the page aloud, you may wish to show other artworks with obvious subjects. Then ask:

- **What patterns and textures do you see?**
  (Possible response: fuzzy yarn, furry kittens, sharp claws)

Lesson 6

Family Pictures

The **subject** is the main idea of an artwork.

What kind of family is the subject of this painting?

Artist unknown. *Cat and Kittens*, ca. 1872–1883. Millboard, 11¾ by 13¾ inches. National Gallery of Art, Washington, D.C., gift of Edgar William and Bernice Chrysler Garbisch. Photograph © 1997 Board of Trustees, National Gallery of Art.

52

 Art Background

Art History The painting *Cat and Kittens* is an example of nineteenth century American folk or primitive art created by unknown tradesmen with little or no artistic training. These artworks were once considered to be inferior art, but eventually appealed to twentieth century abstract artists who admired their honest simplicity.

ESL Notes

Use photographs to teach children the names of family members, such as *brother, sister, grandmother, pet.* Encourage them to use these words as they tell about families from books or television.

Studio 6

Draw a Family

1 Plan.

2 Draw.

3 Pick textures.

4 Rub.

Think Like an Artist

How did you make your subject interesting?

53

2 Create

Tell children they will draw a family and then fill in the shapes with rubbings of different textures.

Invite children to look at the pictures as you point to and read the steps. Ask volunteers to describe how they will make their drawing.

In Step 1, ask children to tell a partner how many people (and pets) they will draw. In Step 2, remind them to use most of the paper to draw the figures.

Technique Tip To help children match up shapes on their drawings with the textured object underneath, suggest that they feel the object through the paper *before* they begin a rubbing.

Quick Studio Children can use light-colored crayons to make a background of rubbings first, and then draw their figures on top of it.

3 Close

Have children use the *Think Like an Artist* question to express ideas about their own work. (Possible response: I made people's clothes look like they had textures.)

Ongoing Assessment

If . . . children find they do not have room within their figures to make rubbings,

then . . . suggest that they fill in the background paper with textures instead.

See page 36 from **Unit-by-Unit Resources** for a rubric to assess this studio.

 Fine Arts Connection

Theatre Have children role-play different family members from a favorite book or television program. Encourage other children to guess what member of the family is being role-played by looking at gestures and listening to what is said. Remind children that pets can also be members of a family.

 Meeting Individual Needs

Extend Have children draw an animal family playing together. Then have them fill in the shapes by making rubbings.

Artist at Work

Artist at Work

Kaleidoscopes

Carolyn Bennett made her first kaleidoscope when she was just nine years old. Now it's her job.

Carolyn Bennett

54

At a Glance

Objectives

- Explore a career related to art.
- Identify the use of art in everyday life.
- Relate art to personal experiences.

Materials

- kaleidoscopes
- Sketchbook Journals

NVAS (K–4) #6 Making connections between visual arts and other disciplines

Explore

Display a kaleidoscope and ask volunteers to tell, or show, how it works. If possible, have several inexpensive kaleidoscopes on hand so that every child can have a turn looking through one. Ask: **Where can you find a kaleidoscope in your everyday life?** (Possible response: in gift shops)

Discuss

Read aloud pages 54 and 55. Help children relate the photograph of Bennett in her studio to the kaleidoscopes shown. Ask:

- **If we opened a kaleidoscope, what would be inside?** (Possible response: mirrors, beads)
- **What do you think Bennett likes about her job?** (Possible response: making something beautiful that changes all the time)
- **People spend money to buy kaleidoscopes from her. What do you think they do with them?** (Possible responses: give them as gifts, collect them)

 Career Research

Invite a craftsperson to visit the class and talk about his or her hobby or career. If possible, have the visitor demonstrate how the craft is done. For example, a basket weaver can bring materials to weave a simple mat for children to see what is involved. Before the visit, have children think of questions to ask the visitor.

To make a kaleidoscope,

Bennett tapes mirrors in a tube.

Then she adds beads and other objects.

When you look in the tube

and turn the bottom,

the beads make colorful

shapes and patterns!

55

Apply

Reread pages 54–55. Tell children to pretend that their job is to make kaleidoscopes. Ask them to brainstorm a list of materials that would be interesting to look at if they were placed inside a kaleidoscope. Work with children to create a numbered list like the one below.

Kaleidoscope Materials

1. colorful beads
2. shiny mirrors
3. glitter
4. game pieces
5. plastic shapes

Close

Review the list with children and ask: **What would happen if you forgot to put a variety of colors inside your kaleidoscope?** (Possible response: The patterns inside the kaleidoscope would not be very colorful and people may not want to play with it.)

Sketchbook Journal Invite children to draw the shapes and colors that they might see inside a kaleidoscope.

 Reading Strategy

Identify Cause and Effect Relationships Tell children that as they read or are being read to, they can identify cause and effect relationships. For instance, have children listen for what happens when the bottom of a kaleidoscope is turned. Then reread pages 54 and 55 with children. Have them explain that the colors change and make new patterns. Continue reviewing cause and effect relationships with other information in the text.

Portfolio Project

Portfolio Project

At a Glance

Objectives

• Develop and organize ideas from the environment.

• Demonstrate knowledge of textures and colors.

• Evaluate original artworks by self and peers.

Materials

• small plastic models of animals (optional)

• muffin tins of red, blue, yellow, orange, violet, and green paint; paintbrushes; drawing paper; newsprint; baby food jars of water; paper towels; scissors ⚠; crayons; flat, textured objects; paste or glue

• Rubric 2 from **Unit-by-Unit Resources**

NVAS (K–4) #1 Understanding and applying media, techniques, and processes

NVAS (K–4) #3 Choosing and evaluating a range of subject matter, symbols, and ideas

NVAS (K–4) #5 Reflecting upon and assessing the characteristics and merits of their work and the work of others

Paint Animals with Texture

① **Paint.**

② **Cut.**

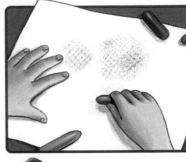
③ **Rub.**

④ **Paste.**

56

Plan

Explain to children that they will create an animal picture with paints, scissors, crayons, and paste. Display small plastic animals and invite children to brainstorm animals to paint as their subject. Then ask:

• **What will you show on your animal?**

Have children think about colors and textures they can add to make their animal distinctive.

Quick Project

Have children make pattern rubbings on newsprint. Then have children cut animal shapes from the newsprint.

👫👫 **Meeting Individual Needs**

Reteach Have children complete the project in several sessions so they can focus on just one step in the process. Always review what they have already done in previous steps and what they are going to do that day.

Extend Let children choose their own textures to rub for their background scene. For example, they might make a rubbing of the bottom of their shoe.

Look at these animals.

Sarah, Age 4. *The Zoo*. Tempera and texture rubbing.

Rachel, Age 5. *Ladybug*. Tempera and texture rubbing.

Share Your Art

1. Tell about the textures you used.

2. Which part would you like to try again? Why?

57

 Gallery Options

Multimedia Show Invite children to hold an art show in which they dress up to resemble the animal they painted. Costumes can be as simple as a pair of paper ears taped on a headband, a tail made from cotton balls or yarn, or a paper-plate mask. Invite another class to view the displayed art, mingle with the "animals," and try to guess which painting belongs to which child.

Create

Gather the materials and guide children through the steps on page 56 to complete the project.

- Remind children to paint a big figure for their animal so the textures will show.
- Encourage children to help each other cut out their animals. You may need to help them cut around tricky parts, such as thin legs or tails.
- In Step 3, children choose textures to make rubbings on a large sheet of newsprint. The rubbings will be the background, or scene, for the painted animal.
- Remind children to put the paste on the back of the animal cutout, not on the sheet of newsprint.

Complete this project in two or three sessions, since children will need to wait until the paint is dry before they cut out their animal.

Close

Point out the artworks from children's portfolios on page 57. Ask:

- **What is the subject of each artwork?** (a mouse, a ladybug)
- **What textures and colors do you see in these artworks?** (bumpy and smooth textures)
- **How are these artworks like yours? How are they different?** (Answers will vary.)

Use the *Share Your Art* questions to help children express ideas about their own artwork. (Answers will vary.)

See page 36 from **Unit-by-Unit Resources** for a rubric to assess this project.

Unit 2 Review

At a Glance

Objectives

- Relate art terms to the environment.
- Identify subject, texture, and pattern in artworks.
- Describe, analyze, interpret, and judge an artwork.

Materials

- **Art Print 8**
- children's art portfolios

NVAS (K–4) #1 Understanding and applying media, techniques, and processes

NVAS (K–4) #2 Using knowledge of structures and functions

NVAS (K–4) #5 Reflecting upon and assessing the characteristics and merits of their work and the work of others

Think About Art

Responses:

color wheel (Point to the color wheel.)
subject (Point to the still life.)
pattern (Point to the patterns of shapes.)
paintbrush (Point to the paintbrush.)

Talk About Art

Pair children to look at each other's portfolios. Guide them to express ideas about their own portfolios as well as their partner's. Model by saying: **I like the artworks in Cameron's portfolio. He used different patterns in them.**

Prompt children to also use words such as *subject* and *texture* to express ideas about their artworks and the artworks of their peers.

 Think About Art

Find a picture for each word.

| color wheel | subject |
| pattern | paintbrush |

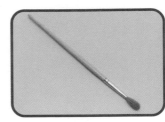 

 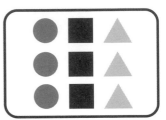

 Talk About Art

- Choose your favorite artwork.
- Tell a friend why you chose it.
- Listen to a friend tell about an artwork.

58

 Assessment Options

Options for assessing children appear in the **Unit-by-Unit Resources.**

- Use the **Vocabulary Worksheets** on pages 29–32 for an informal assessment of Unit 2 vocabulary.
- Use the **Unit 2 Test** on pages 37–40 to assess children's mastery of unit vocabulary and concepts.

Edward Hicks. *The Peaceable Kingdom,* ca. 1840–1845. Oil on canvas, 18 by 24⅛ inches. Brooklyn Museum of Art, Dick S. Ramsay Fund. 40.340.

Put It All Together

1. What looks like it has soft texture?
2. Where is a pattern in this painting?
3. What might the cow see or hear?
4. Do you like the title? Explain.

59

Put It All Together

Use the questions on page 59 to express ideas about the artwork. Possible responses follow.

1. the animals' fur, the lion's mane, the clouds
   DESCRIBE
2. in the cat's fur in the foreground ANALYZE
3. the other animals and hear lambs bleating
   INTERPRET
4. Yes, because the painting looks peaceful. JUDGE

 Art Background

About the Artist American folk artist and Quaker minister Edward Hicks (1780–1849) learned to paint as an apprentice to a coach builder. He went on to have his own business decorating signs and furniture along with coaches. This led to his first easel painting, *The Peaceable Kingdom,* whose theme he returned to again and again, painting at least sixty versions during his lifetime.

Unit 3 Overview

In this unit, children will learn about three-dimensional artworks that take up space. They will also create their own sculptures, puppets, and other forms.

	Unit Opener, p. 60	Lesson 1, p. 62 **Going Around Forms** **Studio 1, p. 63** **Make Paper Forms**	Lesson 2, p. 64 **Animal Forms** **Studio 2, p. 65** **Work with Clay**	Lesson 3, p. 66 **Forms Take Up Space** **Studio 3, p. 67** **Sculpt Yourself**	Look and Compare, p. 68 **Sculpted Families**
Artworks	**Marisol Escobar.** *The Generals,* 1961–1962.		**Artist unknown,** Nigerian. *Pair of Ivory Leopards,* 19th century.	**Artist unknown,** western Mexico, Nayarit. *Musicians,* date unknown.	**Marisol Escobar.** *The Family,* 1962. **Faith Ringgold.** *Mrs. Jones and Family,* 1973.
Vocabulary		form	sculptures		
Materials	• **Art Print 9** • **Instructional Prints**	• small garden sculpture (optional) • paper scraps, pencils, construction paper, glue, tape, clean styrofoam meat trays	modeling clay	• modeling clay • garlic presses, toothpicks ⚠	**Art Prints 9, 10, 11**
Connections	**Home Connection** 3-D sculptures at home **Bookshelf** *Ecology Crafts for Kids* by Bobbe Needham, Sterling, Inc., 1998	**Visual Culture** Forms in sports **ESL Notes** **Fine Arts Connection** Theatre: play Statues **Meeting Individual Needs** Extend	**ESL Notes** **Curriculum Connection** Math: manipulate forms **Meeting Individual Needs** Inclusion	**ESL Notes** **Fine Arts Connection** Dance: Do the Hokey Pokey **Meeting Individual Needs** Reteach	**Reading Strategy** Build background
Assessment Opportunities		Rubric 3 from **Unit-by-Unit Resources** Ongoing Assessment	Rubric 3 from **Unit-by-Unit Resources** Ongoing Assessment	Rubric 3 from **Unit-by-Unit Resources** Ongoing Assessment	

Lesson 4, p. 70 Puppets Studio 4, p. 71 Make a Puppet	Lesson 5, p. 72 Imagination Studio 5, p. 73 Build a Form	Lesson 6, p. 74 Recycle Studio 6, p. 75 Make a Foil Sculpture	Artist at Work, p. 76 Mobiles	Portfolio Project, p. 78 Make Animals	Unit Review, p. 80
Various artists, Bahia, Brazil. *Mamulengo Puppets,* 1994.	**Deborah Butterfield.** *Untitled (Eclipse),* 1986.	**Artist unknown.** *Bottle Cap Giraffe,* 1966.	**Gabe Stoner and Mike Hatton.** *Vito Calzone,* 1999.		**Felipe Benito Archuleta.** *Rooster,* 1986.
puppets	imagination	recycle	mobiles		
• hand puppet, completed wiggle-nose puppet • small plastic cups, adult scissors ⚠, thin glue, tissue paper, child-size scissors ⚠, construction paper scraps, small paintbrushes, markers	• modeling clay; small natural objects such as acorns, pebbles, twigs, leaves; containers	• rubber band ball • toilet paper tubes, aluminum foil, scissors ⚠, glue, construction paper	• mobile • Sketchbook Journals	• photographs of animals (optional) • found objects, such as fabric scraps, buttons, yarn, foam peanuts, craft sticks, cardboard tubes and small boxes, used foil, and so on • scissors ⚠ • glue, tape	• **Art Print 12** • children's art porfolios
ESL Notes	**ESL Notes**	**ESL Notes**	**Community Connection** Mobiles throughout school **Reading Strategy** Use parts of a book to locate information	**Gallery Options** Sculptures on parade **Meeting Individual Needs** Reteach, Extend	
Curriculum Connection Social Studies: puppetry around the world **Meeting Individual Needs** Inclusion	**Curriculum Connection** Music: songs about horses **Meeting Individual Needs** Extend	**Curriculum Connection** Social Studies: recycle paper **Meeting Individual Needs** Inclusion			
Rubric 3 from **Unit-by-Unit Resources** Ongoing Assessment	Rubric 3 from **Unit-by-Unit Resources** Ongoing Assessment	Rubric 3 from **Unit-by-Unit Resources** Ongoing Assessment		Rubric 3 from **Unit-by-Unit Resources**	**Unit-by-Unit Resources** Vocabulary Worksheets, pp. 47–50 Unit 3 Test, pp. 55–58

Unit 3

At a Glance

Objectives

• Identify elements of art in artworks.
• Relate art to personal experiences.
• Respond to and make judgments about artworks.

Materials

• **Art Print 9**

NVAS (K–4) #4 Understanding the visual arts in relation to history and cultures

NVAS (K–4) #5 Reflecting upon and assessing the characteristics and merits of their work and the work of others

NVAS (K–4) #6 Making connections between visual arts and other disciplines

Introduce the Unit

Read the unit title. Tell children that in this unit they will learn about artworks that they can go around. Explain to children that when you are able to go around an object, then you can see all sides of it. Ask children to name other objects that they can go around, such as toys, furniture, and people. Ask: **How can you use your senses to learn about these objects?** (Possible response: I can see all around the objects and touch them with my fingers.)

Display page 60 and talk about the artwork. Tell children it shows two generals—people who lead soldiers. Have children express any other ideas they have about the artwork.

Then invite children to clap a hoof-beat rhythm as you say the words in "Ride the Horse." Say the chant several times so that children can join in.

Help children relate the words in the chant to the sculpture of the generals. Ask:

• **How did the artist make the riders look like generals?** (by giving them hats, boots, square shoulders with epaulets, and stern faces)
• **Do you think the horse can move? How?** (Yes. It has rollers on the bottom of its feet.)

Marisol Escobar. *The Generals*, 1961–1962. Wood and mixed media, 87 by 28½ by 76 inches. Albright-Knox Art Gallery, Buffalo, NY. Gift of Seymour H. Knox, 1962. © 1998 Marisol Escobar/Licensed by VAGA, New York, NY.

60

 Art Background

The Generals In this sculpture by Marisol Escobar (1930–), we see George Washington and Simón Bolívar riding a barrel-shaped horse on castors. To add to the fun, the sculptor built in a phonograph that plays military tunes. Note the contrasts between the angular, blocky figures and the rounded horse.

 Home Connection

Tell children that in this unit, they will be making artworks that can be seen from more than one side. Encourage them to look for things in their home that they might use in a three-dimensional artwork, such as clay or modeling dough, pieces of scrap wood, and so on.

Art Forms

Ride the Horse

Clippity-clop, clippity-clop,

Here we come riding.

Clippity-clop, clippity-clop,

Make a way for us.

Meet the Artist

Marisol Escobar has fun when she makes art. Sometimes she even shows herself as a figure in her artworks!

61

 Bookshelf

Ecology Crafts for Kids
by Bobbe Needham
Sterling, Inc., 1998

Steps for making earth-friendly craft items are shown in photographs as well as text. Projects include gourd birdhouses, sand candles, and paper beads. Some projects require adult help.

Discuss Unit Concepts

Point to the photograph of Marisol Escobar on page 61 and tell children that she is the artist who created *The Generals*. After reading the information about her, tell children that in this unit they will learn about other artists who make artworks they can go around, or see from more than one side.

As you introduce the elements of art and principles of design in Unit 3, you may wish to display the **Instructional Prints.** A print is provided for each element and principle.

Meet the Artist

Marisol Escobar (1930–) was born in Paris to Venezuelan parents. Inspired by pre-Columbian and early American folk art, Marisol has constructed many sculptures from wood, fabric, and terra cotta. In the 1960s she became part of the Pop Art movement and began to incorporate casts of her own face and body parts, as well as everyday objects, onto wooden block-like forms. Her multimedia sculptures are described as witty and satirical, poking fun at different aspects of American society.

Lesson 1

At a Glance

Objectives

- Identify and describe forms in the environment.
- Manipulate paper to create forms in an artwork.
- Respond to and make judgments about artworks.

Materials

- small garden sculpture (optional)
- paper scraps, pencils, construction paper, glue, tape, clean styrofoam meat trays
- Rubric 3 from **Unit-by-Unit Resources**

Vocabulary

form

NVAS (K–4) #1 Understanding and applying media, techniques, and processes

NVAS (K–4) #2 Using knowledge of structures and functions

NVAS (K–4) #3 Choosing and evaluating a range of subject matter, symbols, and ideas

NVAS (K–4) #6 Making connections between visual arts and other disciplines

 Teach

Invite volunteers to tell about gardens, parks, or museums they have visited that contain artworks. Display a small sculpture, if available, and use it to help children understand that, unlike a painting, it can be seen from all sides. Have children share any of their experiences with sculptures or forms. Identify other forms in the classroom. Then have children imagine they are in the photograph as you read page 62 aloud. Ask:

- **How is this artwork different from a painting?** (You can see it from more than one side.)
- **What might the girl be thinking about?** (Possible responses: the story about three animal musicians, the size or weight of the sculpture)

Going Around Forms

A **form** is something you can go around.
Some artists create very large forms.

Gerhard Marcks. *The Bremen Town Musicians*, 1951. Bronze. Located on the west side of the Rathous. Bremen, Germany.

62

 Visual Culture

Invite children to name sports they know about or like to play. Then have them think of forms they use to play the sport, such as bats, balls, shoes, helmets, and so on. Talk about why each object has a particular shape; for example, a soccer ball is round so that it can roll.

ESL Notes

Place a box in the middle of the group and give each child a small doll or other form. Give short commands that include position words. Say, for example: **Joe, put your man inside the box. Carmen, put your doll next to the box.** Children can also respond to questions about an object: **Carmen, is the car on the box?**

Make Paper Forms

Studio 1

1 Fold.

2 Roll.

3 Arrange.

4 Tape.

Art in My World

Find forms on the playground.

63

 Fine Arts Connection

Theatre Tell children that their bodies are forms too. Then play Statues to let children experiment with making forms. Tell children they will have some time to move as you play music or beat a drum. When the music stops, they freeze. Point out interesting forms children make with their bodies.

 Meeting Individual Needs

Extend Show children how to cut fringed or scalloped edges on their forms to create more interest. They can also experiment with long, narrow paper scraps to make "curls."

2 Create

Tell children they will use paper and tape to create forms for an artwork. Have them look at the pictures as you point to and read the steps. Demonstrate how to fold and roll paper scraps to make interesting forms. Continue by modeling how to arrange the forms intuitively. In Step 4, children can help each other cut and use tape to attach their forms to a meat tray.

Technique Tip Show children how to fold small tabs on the bottom of a form if they need a flat surface on which to attach the tape.

Quick Studio Have children work with a partner to make four different forms. They can take turns arranging them on a tabletop.

3 Close

Use the *Art in My World* activity to help children become more aware of art in their surroundings.

Ongoing Assessment

If . . . children have trouble attaching the forms to the foam meat tray,

then . . . have a volunteer or aide pre-cut pieces of tape that are long enough to do the job.

See page 54 from **Unit-by-Unit Resources** for a rubric to assess this studio.

Lesson 2

At a Glance

Objectives

- Identify and discuss sculptures.
- Use modeling clay to make a sculpture.
- Respond to and make judgments about artworks.

Materials

- modeling clay
- Rubric 3 from **Unit-by-Unit Resources**

Vocabulary

sculptures

NVAS (K–4) #1 Understanding and applying media, techniques, and processes

NVAS (K–4) #2 Using knowledge of structures and functions

NVAS (K–4) #3 Choosing and evaluating a range of subject matter, symbols, and ideas

① Teach

Ask volunteers to tell about things they have made from clay or modeling dough. Lead them in a pantomime of pushing, pulling, and shaping the clay.

Display and read aloud page 64. Explain to children that sculptures are made with many types of materials, such as clay. Tell children these sculptures were made in Africa. They were made from ivory. Ask:

- **Could you see these leopards from behind and from the side? How do you know?** (Yes, because they are sculptures.)
- **Why do you think the artist chose to make leopards instead of another animal?** (Possible response: because leopards are African animals)
- **What is your favorite part about these sculptures?** (Answers will vary.)

64

Animal Forms

Some artworks are **sculptures.**

A sculpture is an artwork you can see from all sides.

Artist unknown, Nigerian. *Pair of Ivory Leopards*, 19th century. Ivory and copper, 34⁹⁄₁₆ by 18½ inches (left), 37⁷⁄₁₆ by 18½ inches (right). By kind permission of The Lord Chamberlain's Office, image supplied by The Trustees of the British Museum, London.

64

 Art Background

Art and Culture These ivory and copper leopards from Benin, Nigeria, would be placed on either side of the Oba's, or King's, throne when he sat in state. The king once had live tame leopards at court that had their own special keeper. They would accompany the king on processionals through the city.

 Notes

Give each child a lump of clay. Invite them to respond to commands that you model with your own clay: **I have clay. I push it like this. I pull it like this. Alex, show me how you roll your clay.** Encourage children to repeat your sentences as they follow along.

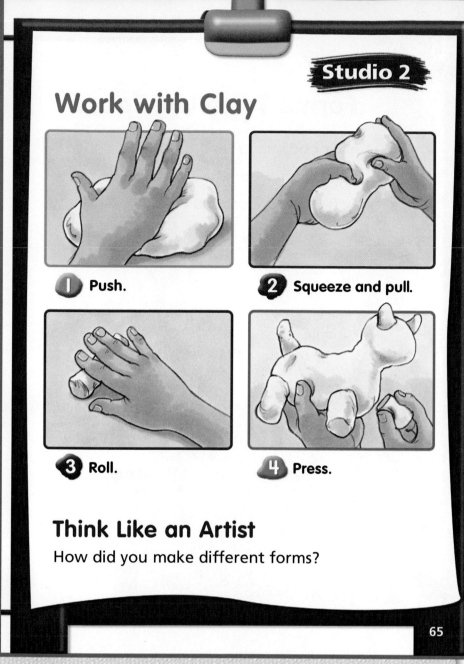

Work with Clay

Studio 2

1. **Push.**

2. **Squeeze and pull.**

3. **Roll.**

4. **Press.**

Think Like an Artist

How did you make different forms?

65

② Create

Explain to children that they will experiment with clay to make forms that they can use in a sculpture.

Invite children to look at the pictures as you point to and read the steps. If you use several colors of clay, tell children to work with the colors separately to keep them bright. Suggest to children that they make their sculpture by arranging and attaching smaller forms together.

Technique Tip Show children how to attach two pieces of clay by smoothing the ends together.

⏱ **Quick Studio** Have children make a sphere, a cube, and a cylinder, and then combine them into a sculpture.

③ Close

Have children use the *Think Like an Artist* question to reflect on their own work. (Possible responses: I pushed, pulled, and rolled the clay.)

Ongoing Assessment

If . . . children's modeling clay becomes dry or crumbly,

then . . . let them wet their fingers to work with the clay.

See page 54 from **Unit-by-Unit Resources** for a rubric to assess this studio.

 Curriculum Connection

Math Make available a variety of forms, such as spheres or wheels, pyramids or cones, and various boxes and cubes. Children can manipulate the objects to find out which ones they can roll, which ones they can stack, and so on.

 Meeting Individual Needs

Inclusion For children who are hearing impaired, model the steps in the Studio with an actual piece of clay. You may wish to place your hand over the child's to guide him or her in pushing, pulling, and rolling the clay.

Lesson 3

At a Glance

Objectives

- Identify and describe space in artworks.
- Use clay to make a human figure.
- Respond to and make judgments about artworks.

Materials

- modeling clay
- garlic presses, toothpicks ⚠ⓢ
- Rubric 3 from **Unit-by-Unit Resources**

Vocabulary

space

NVAS (K–4) #1 Understanding and applying media, techniques, and processes

NVAS (K–4) #2 Using knowledge of structures and functions

NVAS (K–4) #3 Choosing and evaluating a range of subject matter, symbols, and ideas

NVAS (K–4) #6 Making connections between visual arts and other disciplines

❶ Teach

Hold up your hand and have children do the same. Explain to children that your hand takes up space. Use exaggerated movements with your finger to point to the space around your hand and in between your fingers. Then say that there is space all around your hand as well. Have children point to the space around their own hands.

Display page 66 and invite children's comments about the clay figures. After reading the text aloud, further discuss the idea that forms take up space and have space around them. Then ask:

- **What part of the sculpture fills the most space?** (The musicians take up the most space in the sculpture.)
- **Tell a story about this sculpture.** (Possible response: The sculpture is about three musicians playing a song.)

Lesson 3

Forms Take Up Space

Your body takes up **space.**

Space is around it, too.

Point to space around this form.

Artist unknown. Western Mexico, Nayarit. *Musicians*, date unknown. Buff slip with cream and red, 6 ½ by 6 ½ by 3 ½ inches. Los Angeles County Museum of Art, The Proctor Stafford Collection, Museum purchase with Balch Funds. © 1997 Museum Associates, Los Angeles County Museum of Art. All rights reserved.

66

🎨 Art Background

Art and Culture Unlike Aztec or Mayan sculpture, much of which is religious, pre-Columbian Nayarit sculpture is noted for its depiction of men, women, and children going about their daily lives. These small statues were made from clay in Nayarit, a mountainous state in west-central Mexico.

ESL Notes

With a puppet, play a game of Simon Says to help children explore the space around their bodies. Have the puppet say and model commands such as: **Simon says, "Raise your arms in space." Simon says, "Twist around in space."** Encourage children to repeat commands after you.

Sculpt Yourself

1. Squeeze. Pull.
2. Roll.
3. Press.
4. Scratch.

Think Like an Artist

Where is the space around your sculpture?

67

② Create

Explain to children that they will make sculptures of themselves using a variety of clay forms. Invite them to look at the pictures as you point to and read the steps. Ask a volunteer to demonstrate how to use a garlic press to make hair. Show children how to roll separate body parts and then join them to a main form, or torso.

Technique Tip Children can add details to their figures by scratching the clay with toothpicks or scoring it with dull knives.

Quick Studio Instead of attaching body parts to a main form, have children pinch and pull legs, head, and arms from the central lump of clay.

③ Close

Have children use the *Think Like an Artist* question to reflect on their own work. (Possible response: over, under, and beside my body)

Ongoing Assessment

If . . . children have trouble with arms or legs falling off or drooping,

then . . . tell them they can start over with less clay or shorter arms and legs.

See page 54 from **Unit-by-Unit Resources** for a rubric to assess this studio.

 Fine Arts Connection

Dance Tell children that dancers are very aware of the space they move through. Invite them to play a simple movement game such as Hokey Pokey, and encourage them to dance in different ways as they do the Hokey Pokey.

 Meeting Individual Needs

Reteach Before the Studio, have children look in a mirror to describe body parts and their relation to each other. Talk about parts that are round (head, eyes), parts that are long (legs, arms), and parts that are small (fingers, ears, etc.).

Look and Compare

Look and Compare

At a Glance

Objectives

- Compare and contrast two artworks about the same subject.
- Respond to and make judgments about artworks.

Materials

- Art Prints 9, 10, 11

NVAS (K–4) #4 Understanding the visual arts in relation to history and cultures

NVAS (K–4) #5 Reflecting upon and assessing the characteristics and merits of their work and the work of others

Explore

Display **Art Print 9,** *The Generals.* Help children recall this sculpture by Marisol Escobar from page 60. As children look at the two artworks on pages 68 and 69, invite them to predict which one was also created by Marisol and give reasons for their answer. (*The Family;* it is also made of wood; the people look stiff and stern, like the generals.)

Discuss

Read aloud pages 68 and 69. To discuss the artworks, have children focus on the texture and subject of each sculpture. First, have children compare the hard and bold texture of Marisol's sculpture to the soft, brightly colored sculpture by Faith Ringgold. Then have children identify the simple subject of each artwork. Explain that both Marisol's and Ringgold's sculptures show a family. Invite children to share any further ideas about the two artworks. Remind children to show respect for their classmates who have differing opinions.

Sculpted Families

Marisol Escobar. *The Family,* 1962. Painted wood and other materials in three sections, overall, 82⅜ by 65½ by 15½ inches. The Museum of Modern Art, New York. Advisory Committee Fund. Photograph © 1996 The Museum of Modern Art, New York.

Family members work and play.

Artists show how each family is special.

Tell a story about this family.

68

 Art Background

The Family Marisol's bold style is evident in this depiction of a dust-bowl family. As in many of her assemblages, she has used wooden block-like torsos for the grouping and added everyday objects such as a pair of doors. The quiet dignity expressed on the faces reveals the artist's concern and respect for disadvantaged groups.

Mrs. Jones and Family Faith Ringgold (1930–) combines painting, quilting, soft sculpture, and performance art to build awareness of issues facing women and African Americans. Her three-dimensional works include life-sized soft sculptures that feature African-inspired masks.

Faith Ringgold. *Mrs. Jones and Family*, 1973. Canvas fabric pointed and embroidered, 60 by 12 by 16 inches. © Faith Ringgold, Inc. Collection of the artist. Photograph by Karen Bell.

This artist showed a family.

She made a sculpture, too.

How are these sculptures the same?

69

 Reading Strategy

Build Background Tell children that when they read a story or look at an artwork, it helps if they know something about the subject or the author or artist. That way, they can relate the story or artwork to what they already know.

Tell children that Marisol and Ringgold are women who believe that families are important. Remind children that they already know a lot about families. Reread the text. Then have children suggest that they find ways that the families in these artworks are similar to and different from families they know.

Apply

Draw a Venn diagram like the one below on the chalkboard. Tell children that this graphic organizer is a good way to show how two artworks are the same and different.

To fill in the diagram, suggest that children first compare the artworks, looking for ways they are alike. Fill in the middle section as children suggest ideas. Guide children as they look for differences by suggesting that they focus on the subject of each artwork. Possible responses are shown in blue.

Sculptures of Families

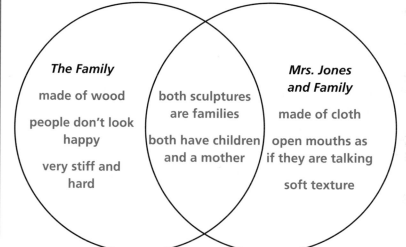

The Family

made of wood

people don't look happy

very stiff and hard

both sculptures are families

both have children and a mother

Mrs. Jones and Family

made of cloth

open mouths as if they are talking

soft texture

Close

Ask children what they learned about artworks that show families. (Possible responses: that all families are alike and different in some ways; that some artists think families are important)

Lesson 4

At a Glance

Objectives

- Identify and describe puppets as forms.
- Use a variety of media to make a puppet.
- Respond to and make judgments about artworks.

Materials

- hand puppet, completed wiggle-nose puppet
- small plastic cups, adult scissors , thin glue, tissue paper, child-size scissors , construction paper scraps, small paintbrushes, markers
- Rubric 3 from **Unit-by-Unit Resources**

Vocabulary

puppets

NVAS (K–4) #1 Understanding and applying media, techniques, and processes
NVAS (K–4) #2 Using knowledge of structures and functions
NVAS (K–4) #3 Choosing and evaluating a range of subject matter, symbols, and ideas
NVAS (K–4) #6 Making connections between visual arts and other disciplines

① Teach

Hide a hand puppet behind your back. Tell children a visitor has come to class to meet them, and then bring out the puppet. Have the puppet talk with children about themselves and their art. Explain to children that puppets, like sculptures, are forms.

Display page 70 and give children time to comment on the puppets' colors, shapes, and textures. Then have children compare them to puppets they have seen or used. Read the page aloud. Ask:

- **Which puppet do you like the most? Why?** (Possible response: I like the middle puppet the best. It reminds me of Pinocchio.)

Puppets

You can tell stories with **puppets.**
These puppets fit over your hand.
Which one do you like best? Why?

Various artists, Bahia, Brazil. *Mamulengo Puppets*, 1994. Painted gourds and papier-mâché heads, cloth, paper, leather, straw bodies, and costumes, each approximately 18 inches in height. "Hands-On" Collection, Education Department, Museum of International Folk Art, a unit of the Museum of New Mexico, Santa Fe, NM.

70

Art Background

Art History Mamulengo puppets are made from gourds and papier-mâché. Originating in Brazil, their name comes from *mano molenga,* meaning limp, floppy hands. They are the Brazilian version of the English puppets Punch and Judy, whose slapstick humor has delighted audiences for generations.

ESL Notes

Give each child a hand puppet or finger puppet, or have partners take turns with one. Model greetings in English, using your puppet: **Hello, Mr. Cat. How are you? My name is _____.** Then have children greet their puppet.

Make a Puppet

Studio 4

1 Paint glue.

2 Decorate.

3 Cut.

4 Draw.

Think Like an Artist

How is your puppet different?

71

2 Create

Cut the nose holes in the plastic cups before children begin working with them.

Show children how a wiggle-nose puppet works and tell them they will make their own. Then point to and read the steps in the process. Explain that in Step 1, they will be painting with glue, not paint. In Step 2, they will arrange pieces of tissue paper onto the wet glue.

Technique Tip In Step 4, let children use markers instead of crayons so that their puppet's features will show up well, and to lessen the chance of tearing the tissue paper.

Quick Studio Have the construction paper pre-cut into eyes, ears, noses, and mouths for children to glue to their cups.

3 Close

Have children use the *Think Like an Artist* question to express ideas about their own work. (Possible response: My puppet has a sad face and a big nose like a clown.)

Ongoing Assessment

If . . . children have trouble with the tissue paper wrinkling and tearing,

then . . . have them simply apply more paper on top of what they already glued down.

See page 54 from **Unit-by-Unit Resources** for a rubric to assess this studio.

 Curriculum Connection

Social Studies Have children research puppetry around the world. They can look on the Internet or go to the library to find books about the subject. Families can contribute puppets for a "Look Only" classroom museum display about puppetry.

 Meeting Individual Needs

Inclusion For children who are visually impaired, have a completed puppet on hand so that they can feel how it is worn on the hand and hear how it "talks." Once children have added visual details to their puppet, have your puppet talk with their puppet.

Lesson 5

At a Glance

Objectives

- Identify and describe how artists use imagination to create artworks.
- Use modeling clay and natural objects to make a form.
- Respond to and make judgments about artworks.

Materials

- modeling clay; small natural objects such as acorns, pebbles, twigs, leaves; containers
- Rubric 3 from **Unit-by-Unit Resources**

Vocabulary

imagination

NVAS (K–4) #1 Understanding and applying media, techniques, and processes

NVAS (K–4) #2 Using knowledge of structures and functions

NVAS (K–4) #3 Choosing and evaluating a range of subject matter, symbols, and ideas

NVAS (K–4) #6 Making connections between visual arts and other disciplines

---

Imagination

Artists use their **imagination.**

They think about things in new ways.

How did this artist use her imagination?

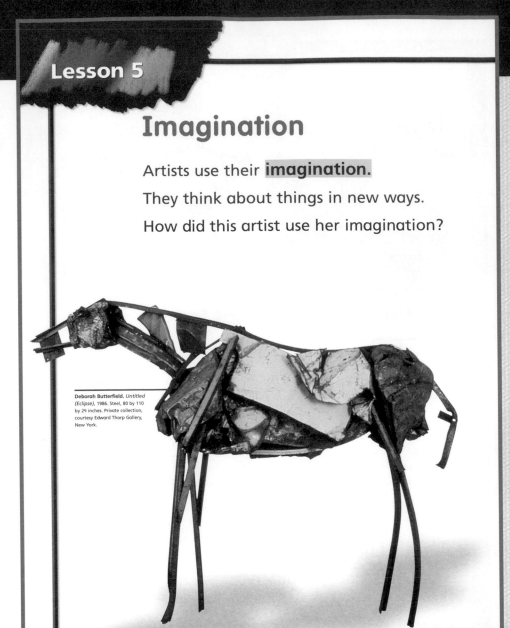

Deborah Butterfield. *Untitled (Eclipse)*, 1986. Steel, 80 by 110 by 24 inches. Private collection, courtesy Edward Thorp Gallery, New York.

72

① Teach

Play a game called Imagination. Whisper an animal name to one child to act out in front of the group. Whoever guesses the animal gets to act out a new animal. Tell children they are using their imagination to play.

Display page 72 and give children time to express ideas about the sculpture. After you read the page aloud, explain to children that when artists use their imagination they create artworks that are unique and different from any other artwork. Ask:

- **How do you know what animal is the subject of this sculpture?** (Possible response: It has long, thin legs like a horse.)
- **How did the artist use her imagination to create this sculpture?** (She used unusual materials to make the horse.)

 Art Background

About the Artist Since childhood, Deborah Butterfield (1949–) has been interested in horses. First working with steel armatures covered with plaster, she sculpted life-sized, realistic horses. Over time, she switched to natural materials like mud and sticks, and then synthetic materials like barbed wire and scrap metal. Her work captures the movements and gestures of the horse.

 Notes

Display photographs of horses and ponies, and have children tell about them. Help them use vocabulary words such as *hoof, mane, tail,* and so on. Let children act out a horse as it eats, trots, and neighs.

72

Build a Form

Studio 5

1 Shape.

2 Choose.

3 Decorate.

4 Scratch.

Think Like an Artist

How did you use your imagination?

73

 Curriculum Connection

Music Teach children a nursery rhyme or a song about horses, such as "Banbury Cross" or "See the Pony Galloping, Galloping." After children have learned the words, they can pretend to be horses moving in rhythm to their singing.

 Meeting Individual Needs

Extend Invite children to build their animal from other materials besides clay. They might like to use metal objects such as paper clips, wire, bottle caps, fasteners, and so on, as Deborah Butterfield did in her sculpture.

2 Create

Tell children they will use their imagination to create an animal sculpture from clay and natural objects.

Invite children to look at the pictures as you point to and read the steps. Brainstorm several creatures, including insects, fish, and birds, so that everyone does not make the same animal.

Technique Tip Review with children how to roll clay to make legs or tails, and how to pinch and pull other body parts from the main form.

Quick Studio Provide children with clay to make a simple geometric form, such as a cube, sphere, or cone. Have children decorate with natural objects.

3 Close

Have children use the *Think Like an Artist* question to reflect on their own work. (Possible response: I pretended that leaves were feathers.)

Ongoing Assessment

If . . . children have trouble imagining how their animal looks in real life,

then . . . suggest that they make another animal or create an imaginary one.

See page 54 from **Unit-by-Unit Resources** for a rubric to assess this studio.

Lesson 6

Lesson 6

At a Glance

Objectives

• Identify and describe recycled objects in artworks.

• Use foil to make a sculpture.

• Respond to and make judgments about artworks.

Materials

• rubber band ball

• toilet paper tubes, aluminum foil, scissors , glue, construction paper

• Rubric 3 from **Unit-by-Unit Resources**

Vocabulary

recycle

NVAS (K–4) #1 Understanding and applying media, techniques, and processes

NVAS (K–4) #2 Using knowledge of structures and functions

NVAS (K–4) #3 Choosing and evaluating a range of subject matter, symbols, and ideas

NVAS (K–4) #6 Making connections between visual arts and other disciplines

Recycle

Artists sometimes **recycle** objects.

They make artworks from old parts.

What did this artist recycle?

Artist unknown. *Bottle Cap Giraffe*, 1966. Carved and painted wood, bottle caps, rubber, glass, fur, and sheet metal, 72 ½ by 54 by 17 ½ inches. National Museum of American Art, Smithsonian Institution, Washington, D.C.

74

① Teach

Show children a rubber band ball. Play a game of Hot Potato using the ball. Tell children that this ball was made by putting together many old, used rubber bands into a ball form. Ask children to name other forms or objects that would make good toys, such as toilet tissue rolls, packing bubbles, and string.

Display page 74 and invite children to express ideas about the artwork. After reading the page aloud, explain to children that some artists create artworks by recycling objects, or reusing old objects. Be sure children understand that the giraffe is mostly made from bottle caps. Then ask:

• **How would the giraffe feel if you could touch it?** (bumpy)

Art Background

Bottle Cap Giraffe This sculpture is covered in bottle caps from three countries and from thirty-four beverage companies. The unknown artist who made it was a true recycler, because he or she also included painted wood, tree branches, old rubber, and a fur tail.

 Notes

Help children answer yes/no and either/or questions about the sculpture on page 74. For example, ask: **Is this a giraffe or an elephant? Is the giraffe on wheels?** More fluent children can point to part of the sculpture and say a word or sentence about it: **This is its neck.**

Make a Foil Sculpture

Studio 6

1. **Cover.**

2. **Twist.**

3. **Cut.**

4. **Glue.**

Think Like an Artist

What do you like about your sculpture?

75

Curriculum Connection

Social Studies Tell children that much of the paper they use at school can be recycled to use in art projects. Label a container for that purpose and encourage children to use it to recycle construction paper scraps, cardboard, foil, and so on.

Meeting Individual Needs

Inclusion For children who have difficulty with fine motor skills, have them choose a very simple animal to make with foil, such as a snake or a fish. Once they have twisted the simple animal, they may want to try another one, or simply complete Steps 3 and 4 with their snake or fish.

② Create

Tell children they will recycle cardboard tubes and aluminum foil to make an animal sculpture.

After you read the steps, ask children to watch as you demonstrate the first two steps. Cover a tube with foil to make an animal's body, and then twist more foil to make legs, wings, or fins.

Technique Tip Tell children to use enough glue and to hold the head against the foil while they count to ten. Then they can test to see whether the glue has bonded to the foil.

⏱ **Quick Studio** Have children work with a partner to make a foil animal.

③ Close

Have children use the *Think Like an Artist* question to express ideas about their own work. (Possible response: I like the long neck I made for my swan.)

Ongoing Assessment

If . . . children want longer legs for their animals,

then . . . show them how to overlap pieces of foil as they twist them together.

See page 54 from **Unit-by-Unit Resources** for a rubric to assess this studio.

Artist at Work

At a Glance

Objectives

- Read about a career in art.
- Relate art to personal experiences.
- Identify the use of art in everyday life.

Materials

- mobile
- Sketchbook Journals

Vocabulary

mobiles

NVAS (K–4) #5 Reflecting upon and assessing the characteristics and merits of their work and the work of others

NVAS (K–4) #6 Making connections between visual arts and other disciplines

Mobiles

Gabe Stoner and Mike Hatton make **mobiles.**

A mobile is a hanging sculpture.

It moves in the wind.

Gabe Stoner and Mike Hatton, *Vito Calzone,* 1999. Anodized aluminum, 26 by 18 inches. Stoner/Hatton Mobiles. Photo: Jerry Anthony.

76

Explore

Display a mobile and ask a volunteer to show how it moves. Help children understand how the different parts are balanced so that it hangs evenly.

Tell children that mobiles are artworks that people often use to decorate their homes in everyday life. Have them cite examples of mobiles they have seen, such as those in a baby nursery or in a library.

Discuss

Read aloud pages 76 and 77. Help children relate the photograph of Stoner and Hatton in their studio to the mobile *Vito Calzone.* Ask:

- **What is the subject of this artwork?** (It is a trapeze artist swinging on a bar.)
- **What are some things you would need to make a mobile?** (Possible responses: string or wire, scissors, objects to hang, a hook, etc.)
- **Why are stars a good shape for a mobile?** (Possible response: because they are always moving in the sky)

 Community Connection

Take a walk with children to look at mobiles in other classrooms or in common areas in your school. Science, math, and social studies teachers may have had older students make mobiles to demonstrate concepts they are learning in those content areas.

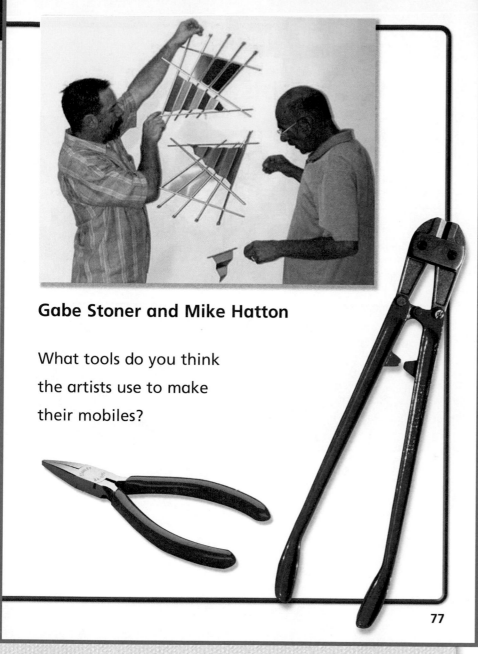

Gabe Stoner and Mike Hatton

What tools do you think
the artists use to make
their mobiles?

77

 Reading Strategy

Use Parts of a Book to Locate Information Tell
children that many books provide pages with information
to help you read and better understand the text. For
instance, the glossary is where you can look to find the
meanings of words.

Reread the text. Say, **What is a sculpture?** After several
volunteers define the word, turn to the *Picture Glossary*.
Ask children to determine if they defined sculpture
correctly based on the picture. Continue by checking
children's understanding of other art terms.

Apply

Ask children to watch as you create a Venn
diagram. Fill in the spaces together as children
share their ideas about mobiles and sculptures.
Possible responses are shown below.

Mobiles and Sculptures

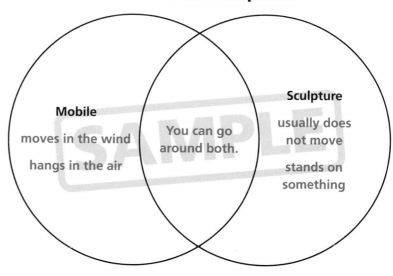

Mobile

moves in the wind

hangs in the air

You can go
around both.

Sculpture

usually does
not move

stands on
something

Close

Review the completed diagram and ask, **If you
were making a mobile, what would be your
subject?** (Possible response: things that fly or
move through the air, like insects or birds)

Sketchbook Journal Invite children to draw
animals or objects that they might see in a mobile.

Portfolio Project

Portfolio Project

At a Glance

Objectives

- Develop and organize ideas from the environment.
- Demonstrate knowledge about forms, sculptures, and space.
- Evaluate original artworks by self and peers.

Materials

- photographs of animals (optional)
- found objects, such as fabric scraps, buttons, yarn, foam peanuts, craft sticks, cardboard tubes and small boxes, used foil, and so on
- scissors ⚠
- glue, tape
- Rubric 3 from **Unit-by-Unit Resources**

NVAS (K–4) #1 Understanding and applying media, techniques, and processes

NVAS (K–4) #3 Choosing and evaluating a range of subject matter, symbols, and ideas

NVAS (K–4) #5 Reflecting upon and assessing the characteristics and merits of their work and the work of others

Make Animals

1 Plan.

2 Tape.

3 Share.

4 Add.

78

Plan

Explain to children that they will create an animal sculpture with everyday objects or recycled objects. Display pictures of animals and invite children to brainstorm animals to make as their subject. Then ask:

- **What animal will you make?**
- **What will you show on your animal?**

Remind children to use their imagination to think of new ways to use recycled objects.

Quick Project

Children can poke or press recycled and everyday items into a lump of clay to make their animal.

Meeting Individual Needs

Reteach Ask children to show you or a partner how they will assemble the parts of their animal before they begin using tape or glue. Be sure their ideas are realistic.

Extend Let a group of children construct a zoo for their animals, coloring cardboard for scenery and using twigs and leaves as imaginary trees and bushes.

What recycled objects do
you see in these sculptures?

Austin, Age 5. *Zebra.*
Multimedia Sculpture.

Kylie, Age 6. *Pretty
Snake.* Multimedia
sculpture.

Share Your Art

1. Point to objects you recycled.
2. Tell a story about your animal.

79

 Gallery Options

Sculptures on Parade Invite children to exhibit their
animal sculptures in a parade through the school. Have
children mount their sculptures on thick cardboard or
plastic trays and carry them in a parade. Have them end
their parade in the library or another classroom in front
of an audience.

Pair each child with a guest and have him or her share
ideas about their peer's artworks in the exhibit. Model
how to express ideas about the exhibition by saying: **The
sculptures in this exhibit use a variety of forms. They are
all unique and original.**

Create

Gather the materials and guide children through
the steps on page 78 to complete the project.
Remind children to create their animals using a
variety of colors and forms.

- In Step 1, encourage children to look at pictures
  of their animal as they plan their artwork.
- Encourage children to help each other arrange
  and attach recycled items to make their animals.
  You may need to help them make thin legs or
  tails.
- Encourage children to share ideas, materials,
  and techniques with each other.
- In Step 4, encourage children to use additional
  recycled materials to make their animal special.

After children finish, help them to write a label for
their animal. They should write a title, their name,
and other information such as the items they used.

Close

Point out the children's art on page 79. Explain to
children that these artworks came from the
portfolios of other kindergartners. Ask:

- **Which recycled objects did each artist use?**
  (Possible response: toilet tissue roll, plastic cups,
  and cotton swabs)
- **How did the artists use their imagination?
  What do you like about their artworks?**
  (Answers will vary.)

Use the *Share Your Art* prompts to help children
express ideas about their own artwork. Encourage
them to also talk about what they like most about
their animal. (Answers will vary.)

See page 54 from **Unit-by-Unit Resources** for a
rubric to assess this project.

Unit 3 Review

At a Glance

Objectives

- Relate art terms to the environment.
- Identify forms and textures in artworks.
- Describe, analyze, interpret, and judge an artwork.

Materials

- **Art Print 12**
- children's art portfolios

NVAS (K–4) #1 Understanding and applying media, techniques, and processes

NVAS (K–4) #2 Using knowledge of structures and functions

NVAS (K–4) #5 Reflecting upon and assessing the characteristics and merits of their work and the work of others

Think About Art

Possible responses:

mobile (Point to the mobile.)
form (Point to the cube, pyramid, and organic shape.)
recycle (Point to the child recycling.)
puppet (Point to the puppet.)

Talk About Art

Prompt children to use words such as *form*, *imagination*, and *recycled* to describe artworks in friends' portfolios. As children share ideas about the work of others, encourage them to show respect for differing opinions.

 ## Think About Art

Match each word with a picture.

mobile   **form**   **recycle**   **puppet**

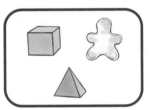

 ## Talk About Art

- Look at your friends' artworks.
- How did they use their imagination?

80

 Assessment Options

Options for assessing children appear in the **Unit-by-Unit Resources.**

- Use the **Vocabulary Worksheets** on pages 47–50 for an informal assessment of Unit 3 vocabulary.
- Use the **Unit 3 Test** on pages 55–58 to assess children's mastery of unit vocabulary and concepts.

Felipe Benito Archuleta. *Rooster*, 1986. Cottonwood, plywood, metal, glue, and sawdust, carved and assembled, 24½ by 7½ by 31½ inches. Photograph by Robert Nugent, courtesy Davis Mather Folk Art Gallery, Santa Fe, NM.

Put It All Together

1. What is the subject of this form?
2. What materials did the artist use?
3. Why do you think the artist made this sculpture?
4. What do you like best about it?

Put It All Together

Use the questions on page 81 to evaluate the artwork. Possible responses follow.

1. a rooster DESCRIBE
2. wood, paint, sawdust, metal, glue ANALYZE
3. to show roosters as he really sees them; to make people smile INTERPRET
4. I like the colors the artist used. JUDGE

 Art Background

About the Artist Felipe Benito Archuleta (1910–1991) was a self-taught artist who began carving animals when he was in his fifties. He drew from the Hispanic tradition in New Mexico of carving saints, or *santos*, and applied the same reverence to the carving of animals. His sculptures are made from native New Mexican cottonwood and found materials such as straw, nails, and marbles.

Unit 4 Overview

Artists often turn to their environments for inspiration for their artworks. As backgrounds, cultures, and environments vary between artists, so do their styles and methods. In this unit, children will learn about various forms of art and the people who make them. They will also create their own artworks using the elements of art and principles of design.

	Unit Opener, p. 82	Lesson 1, p. 84 Photographs Studio 1, p. 85 Collect Photographs	Lesson 2, p. 86 Prints Studio 2, p. 87 Make a Monoprint	Lesson 3, p. 88 Weavers Studio 3, p. 89 Make a Cloth Collage	Look and Compare, p. 90 Places in Artworks
Artworks	 **Vincent van Gogh.** *The Starry Night,* 1889.		 **Utagawa Hiroshige.** *Asakusa Ricefields During the Cock Festival,* 1857.	 **Artist unknown.** *Huipil,* 20th century.	 **Vincent van Gogh.** *The Bedroom at Arles,* 1889. **Edward Hopper.** *Rooms by the Sea,* 1951.
Vocabulary		camera, photograph	print	weavers	
Materials	• Art Print 13 • Instructional Prints	• a photograph and an illustration of the same subject, such as a food or a pet • old magazines, scissors ⚠, glue, construction paper	• stamping tool and ink pad • finger paint, finger painting paper, drawing paper, smocks, spoons, damp rag for wiping hands	• woven cloth or burlap, hand lens (optional) • pencils or crayons, construction paper, fabric and wallpaper scraps, scissors ⚠, glue	Art Prints 13, 14, 15
Connections	**Home Connection** artworks at home **Bookshelf** *Art Dog* by Thacher Hurd, BT Bound, 1999	**Visual Culture** choices in art **ESL Notes** **Curriculum Connection** Social Studies: art in the workplace **Meeting Individual Needs** Inclusion	**ESL Notes** **Fine Arts Connection** Theatre: mirror each other's movements **Meeting Individual Needs** Extend	**ESL Notes** **Curriculum Connection** Social Studies: the art of weaving in everyday life **Meeting Individual Needs** Reteach	**Reading Strategy** Ask questions
Assessment Opportunities		Rubric 4 from **Unit-by-Unit Resources** Ongoing Assessment	Rubric 4 from **Unit-by-Unit Resources** Ongoing Assessment	Rubric 4 from **Unit-by-Unit Resources** Ongoing Assessment	

Lesson 4, p. 92 **Balance** **Studio 4, p. 93** **Make Animal Socks**	Lesson 5, p. 94 **Art and Nature** **Studio 5, p. 95** **Make a Sun Print**	Lesson 6, p. 96 **Movement** **Studio 6, p. 97** **Make a Flip Book**	**Artist at Work, p. 98** **Kites**	**Portfolio Project,** **p. 100** **Sew a Pouch**	**Unit Review, p. 102**
  Artist unknown, Chinese. *Baby's Shoes*, early 20th century.	 **Andy Goldsworthy.** *Rain Shadow*, 1993.	 **Katsushika Hokusai.** *Boy Juggling Shells*, ca. 1800.	 *New Zealand Star Kite* by Jose Sainz.		 **Elizabeth Catlett.** *Baile (Dance)*, 1970.
balance	nature	movement			
• old child-sized socks, glue, scissors ⚠, 3-inch squares of burlap or felt, yarn, sewing scraps	• dark-colored construction paper; natural objects such as acorns, flowers, pebbles, twigs, leaves; trays	• sample flip books; crayons; small rectangular books made with stiff paper, stapled so they open horizontally; pencils (optional)	• kite • Sketchbook Journals	• pocketbook or pouch, tapestry needles with blunt ends and large eyes ⚠, 16-inch lengths of thin yarn • 4½- by 9-inch strips of burlap, 1 per child • sewing scraps, buttons, yarn, sequins or beads • fabric glue • feathers (optional)	• **Art Print 16** • Children's art portfolios
ESL Notes **Fine Arts Connection** Dance: balance in movement **Meeting Individual Needs** Inclusion	**ESL Notes** **Curriculum Connection** Health: sun protection **Meeting Individual Needs** Extend	**ESL Notes** **Fine Arts Connection** Music: differences in tempos **Meeting Individual Needs** Inclusion	**Career Research** Kites and their designers **Reading Strategy** Relate to personal experience	**Gallery Options** Show and tell treasures **Meeting Individual Needs** Reteach, Extend	
Rubric 4 from **Unit-by-Unit Resources** Ongoing Assessment	Rubric 4 from **Unit-by-Unit Resources** Ongoing Assessment	Rubric 4 from **Unit-by-Unit Resources** Ongoing Assessment		Rubric 4 from **Unit-by-Unit Resources**	**Unit-by-Unit Resources** Vocabulary Worksheets, pp. 65–68 Unit 4 Test, pp. 73–76

Unit 4

At a Glance

Objectives

- Identify elements of art and principles of design in artworks.
- Relate art to personal experiences.
- Respond to and make judgments about artworks.

Materials

- Art Print 13

NVAS (K–4) #4 Understanding the visual arts in relation to history and cultures

NVAS (K–4) #5 Reflecting upon and assessing the characteristics and merits of their work and the work of others

Vincent van Gogh. *The Starry Night*, 1889. Oil on canvas, 29 by 36¼ inches. The Museum of Modern Art, New York.

82

Introduce the Unit

Ask children to imagine that it is nighttime. Talk about nighttime with children. Model by saying: **I can see the moon and the stars. I can hear animal sounds.** Continue by asking children to provide more information about nighttime, using their senses.

Then display page 82 and invite children's comments about the painting. Ask them to identify the subject of the artwork. (nighttime) Sing the song "Star" to the tune of "Twinkle, Twinkle, Little Star" several times. Children can point to a star in *The Starry Night* each time they sing the song.

Help children relate the song to the painting. Ask:

- **What lines make the stars twinkle?** (curved and swirling lines)
- **How does this painting make you feel?** (Possible response: It makes me feel happy. I like to look at the stars and the moon at night.)

 Art Background

The Starry Night This painting of the night sky gives us a sense of movement with its thickly painted brushstrokes, glowing stars, and swirling clouds. The village, painted in shorter, orderly brushstrokes, imparts a peaceful, quiet feeling. Unlike many of Van Gogh's paintings, *The Starry Night* was painted from memory.

 Home Connection

Encourage children to investigate objects around their home. Have children find interesting lines, shapes, colors, and textures inside or outside their home. They might want to create an artwork with a family member that shows some things they observe.

A World of Art

Star

Twinkle, twinkle,

Star so bright.

You light up

The sky tonight.

Meet the Artist

Vincent van Gogh used bright colors in his paintings. Many of his paintings were of the outdoors.

Vincent van Gogh. *Self-Portrait,* 1887.

83

Discuss Unit Concepts

Point to the self-portrait of Vincent van Gogh on page 83 and tell children that he is the artist who created *The Starry Night*. Read the information about him and encourage children to speculate why he painted the night sky. (Possible response: Maybe he really liked the outdoors at nighttime.)

Read the title of Unit 4. Tell children that in this unit, they will learn about artists, like Vincent van Gogh, who like to create artworks about the world around them. Ask: **What subjects from the world would you like to create artworks about?**

As you introduce each element of art and principle of design, you may wish to display the **Instructional Prints.** A print is provided for each element and principle.

Meet the Artist

Vincent van Gogh (1853–1890) tried several jobs, including teaching and missionary work, before he became a painter in 1880. His idea that painting should be self-expression appears many times in the hundreds of letters he wrote to his younger brother, Theo. Vincent moved to Paris in 1886 to join Theo, who was in the business of buying and selling paintings. In 1888 the painter moved to Arles in the south of France, hoping to start a community of artists. It was here that Van Gogh painted some of his best known artworks.

 Bookshelf

Art Dog
by Thacher Hurd
BT Bound, 1999

Arthur Dog is a guard at the art museum by day, and by night, a lone artist who signs his giant murals "Art Dog." This fearless, art-loving pooch finds the stolen "Mona Woofa" masterpiece and saves the day!

Lesson 1

At a Glance

Objectives

- Identify and describe photographs.
- Use a variety of media to make a photo collage.
- Respond to and make judgments about artworks.

Materials

- a photograph and an illustration of the same subject, such as a food or a pet
- old magazines, scissors , glue, construction paper
- Rubric 4 from **Unit-by-Unit Resources**

Vocabulary

camera, photograph

NVAS (K–4) #1 Understanding and applying media, techniques, and processes

NVAS (K–4) #2 Using knowledge of structures and functions

NVAS (K–4) #3 Choosing and evaluating a range of subject matter, symbols, and ideas

NVAS (K–4) #6 Making connections between visual arts and other disciplines

① Teach

Show children a photograph and an illustration of the same subject such as an apple or a dog. Invite volunteers to tell how the two pictures are the same and how they are different. (Possible responses: The illustration is someone's idea of how the apple or dog looks; the photograph shows a real apple or dog.)

Discuss with children that some artists like to take photographs because they like realistic subjects. Point out subjects in the environment that would be good to photograph. Model by saying: **If I had a camera, I would take pictures of people and families.** Ask children to identify subjects they would like to photograph.

Lesson 1

Photographs

This girl is using a **camera**.

She is taking a picture, or **photograph**.

Why do you think she chose this subject?

 ### Visual Culture

Show children a variety of photographs, such as family portraits, historical and news photos, and photographs from advertisements. Have children decide which ones they think do a good job of showing their subject, and give reasons for their choices.

ESL Notes

Show children a camera. After talking about it, lead a pantomime about taking pictures and posing for them. Give short commands and model the responses that you expect from children. Say, for example: **Frankie, may I take your picture? Stand still! Smile! Now you take a picture of me.**

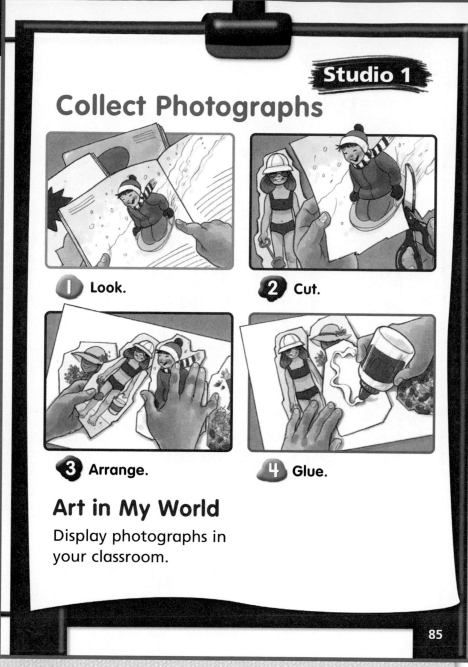

Collect Photographs

Studio 1

1. **Look.**
2. **Cut.**
3. **Arrange.**
4. **Glue.**

Art in My World
Display photographs in your classroom.

② Create

Tell children they will find photographs in old magazines to cut out and arrange in an artwork. Have them look at the pictures as you point to and read the steps.

Point out that the child who made this photo collage had a theme, the seasons. Help children brainstorm possible themes, such as animals, favorite foods, things that are mostly the same color, and so on.

Technique Tip Show children how to slowly and carefully tear a page out of a magazine before trying to cut something out of the page.

Quick Studio Have children work with a partner to make a themed collage. They can take turns cutting and gluing photographs they find.

③ Close

Use the *Art in My World* activity to help children glean information about the world around them.

Ongoing Assessment

If . . . children have trouble finding enough photographs to fit their theme,

then . . . help them choose a broader theme or suggest that they draw additional objects, people, or places in their collage.

See page 72 from **Unit-by-Unit Resources** for a rubric to assess this studio.

 Curriculum Connection

Social Studies Display two or three photographs of very busy places people work, such as a city scene, an office, and a cluttered room in a house. Have partners take turns choosing one thing in one picture to give clues about for the other child to guess or point to.

 Meeting Individual Needs

Inclusion Children who are visually impaired can tell a partner or classroom aide what theme they would like to explore in their photo collage. As the partner finds photographs, the child who is visually impaired can glue them in the collage. Make available textured scraps that he or she can add to the collage if so desired.

Lesson 2

At a Glance

Objectives

• Identify and describe prints.
• Use finger paint to make a monoprint.
• Respond to and make judgments about artworks.

Materials

• stamping tool and ink pad
• finger paint, finger painting paper, drawing paper, smocks, spoons, damp rag for wiping hands
• Rubric 4 from **Unit-by-Unit Resources**

Vocabulary

print

NVAS (K–4) #1 Understanding and applying media, techniques, and processes

NVAS (K–4) #2 Using knowledge of structures and functions

NVAS (K–4) #3 Choosing and evaluating a range of subject matter, symbols, and ideas

NVAS (K–4) #6 Making connections between visual arts and other disciplines

Lesson 2

Prints

This artist carved a picture in wood.
Then he added ink and made a **print.**

Utagawa Hiroshige. *Asakusa Ricefields During the Cock Festival,* 1857. Color print from wood blocks, 13¼ by 8⅞ inches. Fitzwilliam Museum, Cambridge, U.K.

86

① Teach

Display a rubber stamp and an ink pad and ask a volunteer to show or explain how to use them. Point out that with the stamp, you can make the same design or picture as many times as you want.

Display and read aloud page 86. Have children express ideas about Hiroshige's print. Model by saying: **This print shows thick horizontal and vertical lines. I like how the window view shows a lot of land.** Explain that when you make a print like this one, you can make more than one copy. Ask:

• **How can you tell that the cat is indoors?** (It is looking through a window at a distant scene.)

 Art Background

About the Artist Painter and Japanese print artist Utagawa Hiroshige (1797–1858) was part of the *ukiyo-e* ("pictures of the floating world") school of printmaking. He is noted for his woodblock prints of landscapes. Hiroshige dominated printmaking in Japan for the first half of the nineteenth century.

 Notes

Teach children an action song about art, to the tune of "Mulberry Bush": **This is the way we finger paint, finger paint, finger paint . . . etc.** Other verses might talk about drawing with crayons, working with clay, or pulling a print. For each verse, model the actions involved with that particular medium.

86

Make a Monoprint

Studio 2

1. **Spread.**
2. **Draw.**
3. **Press.**
4. **Pull.**

Think Like an Artist

How did you make your print?

87

② Create

Explain that a *monoprint* is a type of print that can only be copied one time. Tell children that they will first paint with their fingers and then make a monoprint of their subject.

Invite children to look at the pictures as you point to and read the steps. Tell them that they should create their artwork using a variety of lines. Then demonstrate the process, emphasizing how lightly you press the paper in Step 3.

Technique Tip Show children how to slowly and carefully peel the paper away from their finger painting with one hand, while holding just the top corners of the drawing paper with the other hand.

Quick Studio Have pairs of children finger paint on a tabletop. Both children can experiment with lines and shapes, and then pull prints.

③ Close

Have children use the *Think Like an Artist* question to reflect on their own work. (Possible responses: I painted with my fingers, pressed a paper onto the paint, and pulled it off. My picture was printed on the paper.)

Ongoing Assessment

If . . . children's prints look empty,

then . . . tell them to pull another print, this time smoothing the entire paper over the image with the palm of their hands.

See page 72 from **Unit-by-Unit Resources** for a rubric to assess this studio.

 **Fine Arts Connection**

Theatre Point out how the monoprint children made was a mirror image of their finger painting. Ask a few volunteers to be your mirror. Sit on the floor facing each other. Begin a very slow, simple movement such as raising your arms over your head. The children should mirror your movements exactly.

Meeting Individual Needs

Extend Have children frame their monoprint. They can staple together four strips of construction paper to make the frame and then use thumbprints to decorate it.

Lesson 3

At a Glance

Objectives

- Identify and describe weaving as an art.
- Use a variety of media to make a cloth collage.
- Respond to and make judgments about artworks.

Materials

- woven cloth or burlap, hand lens (optional)
- pencils or crayons, construction paper, fabric and wallpaper scraps, scissors , glue
- Rubric 4 from **Unit-by-Unit Resources**

Vocabulary

weavers

NVAS (K–4) #1 Understanding and applying media, techniques, and processes

NVAS (K–4) #2 Using knowledge of structures and functions

NVAS (K–4) #3 Choosing and evaluating a range of subject matter, symbols, and ideas

NVAS (K–4) #6 Making connections between visual arts and other disciplines

Lesson 3

Weavers

Some artists are **weavers.**

They weave cloth on a loom.

They weave clothes and blankets.

Artist unknown, Guatemalan. *Huipil*, 20th century. Woven cotton, 28 by 24 inches.

Weaver

88

① Teach

Show children some woven cloth or a piece of burlap. Children can use a hand lens to see how the horizontal and vertical threads go over and under each other to make a tight weave. Point out the texture. Model by saying: **The texture of the cloth is bumpy yet soft.** Have children identify the texture of other woven clothes or cloth.

Display page 88 and read the text aloud. Help children relate the photograph of the weaver to the idea that some rugs, blankets, and clothing are woven on a loom. Ask:

- **Where are some patterns that the weaver made in the vest?** (Children should point to the zigzag lines or repeated colors.)
- **Do you like this vest? Why?** (Possible response: Yes; I like how the artist used zigzag lines.)

Art Background

Art and Culture Modern-day Mayan Indians of Guatemala continue their centuries-old weaving tradition by making *huipils* (women's blouses). Cotton cloth is woven on a simple backstrap loom. Each community has its own design and colors, making these garments an expression of village cultural identity.

ESL Notes

Display a woven basket or a photograph of one in which the weaving is easy to see. Model words or simple sentences such as: **This is a basket. A weaver used red and blue. These blue pieces go up and down. The red pieces go in and out.** Then ask questions such as: **Is this a basket or a box?**

Make a Cloth Collage

Studio 3

1 **Draw.**

2 **Cut.**

3 **Plan.**

4 **Glue.**

Think Like an Artist

Why would your clothing be fun to wear?

89

Curriculum Connection

Social Studies Tell children that many of the clothes they wear in their everyday life is created through the art of weaving. Ask children to identify clothes that have been weaved, such as sweaters, hats, and scarves. Ask them to draw these items by season to make a book that shows and tells what clothing is appropriate for each season.

Meeting Individual Needs

Reteach Before the Studio, have children look in a mirror to describe the clothing they are wearing. Help them decide what clothing they will make for their artwork.

2 Create

Explain to children that they will make pictures of themselves wearing clothing made from fabric scraps.

Invite children to look at the pictures as you point to and read the steps. Show children how to cut through fabric by folding it in half and stretching the fold across the blade of the scissors. The tension on the cloth will help the scissors cut cleanly.

Technique Tip Children who are inexperienced with scissors may need to be shown how to hold them correctly. Be sure that left-handed children have left-handed scissors.

Quick Studio In advance, cut out hat shapes from fabric scraps. Children can choose one to glue at the top of their drawing paper, and then draw a child wearing it.

3 Close

Have children use the *Think Like an Artist* question to express ideas about their own work. (Possible response: It has flowers all over it.) Have children talk about what they like about their collages.

Ongoing Assessment

If . . . children have trouble cutting through fabric,

then . . . suggest that they use wallpaper or felt scraps, which are easier to cut.

See page 72 from **Unit-by-Unit Resources** for a rubric to assess this studio.

Look and Compare

Look and Compare

Places in Artworks

Objectives

- Compare and contrast two artworks about the same subject.
- Respond to and make judgments about artworks.

Materials

- **Art Prints 13, 14, 15**

NVAS (K–4) #4 Understanding the visual arts in relation to history and cultures

NVAS (K–4) #5 Reflecting upon and assessing the characteristics and merits of their work and the work of others

Explore

Display **Art Print 13,** *The Starry Night*. Help children recall this painting by Vincent van Gogh from page 82. As children look at the two artworks on pages 90 and 91, invite them to predict which one was also created by Van Gogh, and give reasons for their answer. (*The Bedroom at Arles* because it also has bright colors and similar kinds of lines.)

Discuss

Read aloud pages 90 and 91. To discuss the artworks, have children focus on the subject of each painting. Tell children that Van Gogh's painting is a cluttered, cramped bedroom. Lead children to describe Hopper's painting as a quiet, nearly empty room.

Children may say they would like to visit the first room because it is cheerful and a little messy, or they might prefer the second one because they could relax there and look at the water. As children share their ideas about the works by these artists, remind them to demonstrate respect for differing opinions by other classmates.

What is the subject of this painting?

Is this bedroom like yours?

How is it different?

Vincent van Gogh. *The Bedroom at Arles,* 1889. Oil on canvas, 23 by 29½ inches. Musée d'Orsay, Paris.

90

 Art Background

The Bedroom at Arles This painting was a personal favorite of the Dutch painter Vincent van Gogh, who painted three versions of the subject. He wanted the colors and the unusual perspective to be restful and suggestive of sleep. As he wrote in a letter, ". . . looking at the picture ought to rest the brain, or rather the imagination."

Rooms by the Sea American painter Edward Hopper (1882–1967) presents us with an empty room lit by a shaft of sunlight from a door that opens directly on the ocean. How light illuminates a subject and creates a mood is an important aspect of Hopper's paintings. In *Rooms by the Sea*, the light actually becomes the subject of the painting.

Edward Hopper. *Rooms by the Sea*, 1951. Oil on canvas, 29 by 40 inches. Yale University Art Gallery, New Haven, CT.

What is the subject of this painting?

How is it different from Van Gogh's?

Which one would you like to visit? Why?

91

Apply

Draw a Venn diagram like the one below on the chalkboard. Tell children that this graphic organizer is a good way to show how two artworks are the same and different.

To fill in the diagram, suggest that children first compare the artworks, looking for ways they are alike. Fill in the middle section as children suggest ideas. Guide children as they look for differences by suggesting that they focus on the objects in the two artworks. Possible responses are shown in blue.

Paintings of Rooms

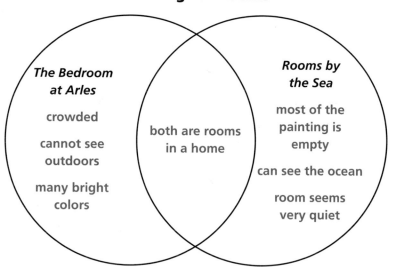

The Bedroom at Arles

crowded

cannot see outdoors

many bright colors

both are rooms in a home

Rooms by the Sea

most of the painting is empty

can see the ocean

room seems very quiet

Close

Ask children what they learned about artworks that show places. (Possible response: The objects that artists choose to show, or not show, can affect how you feel about the subject.)

 Reading Strategy

Ask Questions Create a Vincent van Gogh exhibit in your classroom. Display **Art Print 13**, *The Starry Night* and **Art Print 14**, *The Bedroom at Arles*. Provide other examples of Van Gogh's artworks by displaying artworks in books. Share ideas about the artworks at the exhibit. Model by saying: **Van Gogh's artworks often show thick brushstrokes. There are a variety of lines.** Then have children share their ideas about the exhibit.

Tell children that when they read a story or look at artworks, they should ask questions to get more information. Lead them into asking questions about Van Gogh's artworks in the exhibit, such as: **How are his paintings similar? How are they different?**

Lesson 4

At a Glance

Objectives

- Identify and describe balance.
- Use a variety of media to make animal socks.
- Respond to and make judgments about artworks.

Materials

- old child-sized socks, glue, scissors , 3-inch squares of burlap or felt, yarn, sewing scraps
- Rubric 4 from **Unit-by-Unit Resources**

Vocabulary

balance

NVAS (K–4) #1 Understanding and applying media, techniques, and processes

NVAS (K–4) #2 Using knowledge of structures and functions

NVAS (K–4) #3 Choosing and evaluating a range of subject matter, symbols, and ideas

NVAS (K–4) #6 Making connections between visual arts and other disciplines

❶ Teach

Ask a volunteer to stand in front of the group, legs and arms spread wide. Show children how he or she is balanced, that is, if you drew an imaginary vertical line down the middle of the child, both sides are the same.

Display page 92 and read it aloud. Have children express ideas about *Bag* and *Baby's Shoes*. Point out how *Baby's Shoes* has balance because both sides of each shoe look about the same. Children may say the bag shows balance because if a vertical line was drawn down the middle, both sides would be the same. Ask:

- **Look at one of your shoes. How does it show balance?** (Each side of my shoe looks about the same.)
- **What other objects show balance?** (Possible responses: socks, butterfly wings, leaves)

Balance

These shoes show **balance.**

Both sides are about the same.

Does the pouch show balance? How?

Artist unknown, Chinese. *Baby's Shoes,* early 20th century. Embroidered, appliquéd silk on silk, 1¼ inches high. Girard Foundation Collection at the Museum of International Folk Art, Santa Fe, NM. Photograph by Michel Monteaux.

Artist unknown. *Bag,* ca. 1840. Seneca, New York. Velvet, silk, glass beads, and cotton, 7 by 6¼ inches. The Fenimore Art Museum, Cooperstown, NY.

92

🎨 Art Background

Bag This bag was created by the Seneca Indians of New York. The Seneca Indians inhabited Western New York before the Europeans. Beaded bags, similar to this one, were often sold by Seneca women at tourist places like Niagara Falls.

Baby Shoes The embroidered baby's shoes are appliquéd silk on silk. Chinese tradition asserts that the craft of weaving fabric from silk threads was developed in China as early as the 27th century B.C.

ᴇSL Notes

Invite children to help you build a block structure that is exactly the same on both sides. As you build, talk about how the parts show balance. Say: **This is balanced.** Have children repeat after you.

Studio 4

Make Animal Socks

1. Draw.
2. Cut.
3. Glue.
4. Add.

Think Like an Artist

How does your sock show balance?

93

② Create

Tell children they will make animal socks like the shoes on page 92. Then point to and read the steps in the process. Explain that in Step 3, they will be gluing an animal face onto the top of a pair of socks. When the glue dries, they can wear the socks.

In Step 4, have children use their finger to draw an imaginary line down the middle of the face. This will help children see the balance of their design.

Technique Tip Help children stuff newspapers into their socks so they are easier to work with.

Quick Studio Have children draw the outline of an animal face on a square of black felt, glue yarn on the outline, and then add beads and sequins for facial features.

③ Close

Have children use the *Think Like an Artist* question to express ideas about personal artworks. (Possible response: Each sock looks like the other sock.)

Ongoing Assessment

If . . . children have trouble gluing details on their animal faces,

then . . . have them use water-based markers to draw details instead.

See page 72 from **Unit-by-Unit Resources** for a rubric to assess this studio.

Fine Arts Connection

Dance With a partner, perform a simple dance in which you mirror each other's movements. Afterward, ask children to tell how the two of you showed balance in your steps and movements. Then have children pair off. Partners can practice performing and mirroring each other's movements.

Meeting Individual Needs

Inclusion Offer children the option of making sock puppets to put on their hands instead of animal socks to wear on their feet.

Lesson 5

At a Glance

Objectives

- Use natural objects to make a sun print.
- Respond to and make judgments about artworks.

Materials

- dark-colored construction paper; natural objects such as acorns, flowers, pebbles, twigs, leaves; trays
- Rubric 4 from **Unit-by-Unit Resources**

Vocabulary

nature

NVAS (K–4) #2 Using knowledge of structures and functions

NVAS (K–4) #3 Choosing and evaluating a range of subject matter, symbols, and ideas

NVAS (K–4) #6 Making connections between visual arts and other disciplines

① Teach

Take a walk or look outside the window and tell children that they are exploring *nature*. Explain that nature can mean the outdoors and all the plants and animals that are in it. Then ask children to share information about nature, using their senses.

Display and read page 94. Help children understand that the rain shadow isn't really a shadow. It is the part of the rock that stayed dry in the rain. Ask:

- **Do you think this artist loves nature? How do you know?** (Yes; he made an artwork using just his own body, a rock, and the rain.)
- **What do you think about this artwork?** (Possible response: I like that he used nature to create it.)

Art and Nature

Artists see art in **nature.**

This artist lay on a big rock.

The rain made a rain shadow.

Andy Goldsworthy. *Rain Shadow,* 1993. Central Park, New York. Courtesy of Andy Goldsworthy Studio. © Andy Goldsworthy.

94

 Art Background

About the Artist British artist Andy Goldsworthy (1956–) is a sculptor who transforms natural materials in their own settings. Many of his sculptures are preserved only in photographs because they are made of ephemeral materials such as melting snow, drying rain, blowing leaves, and sand castles at the water's edge.

ESL Notes

Teach children weather words by substituting them for *rainy* in this song, to the tune of "The Muffin Man": **Do you like a rainy day? a rainy day? a rainy day? Do you like a rainy day? Tell me yes or no.** Children can reply with a word, a nod, or with the second verse of the song: **Yes, I like a rainy day, etc.**

Make a Sun Print

1 Choose.

2 Arrange.

3 Wait.

4 Share.

Think Like an Artist

How is your sun print like the *Rain Shadow*?

95

Curriculum Connection

Health Display a pair of sunglasses, a hat, suntan lotion, and a long-sleeved shirt. Ask children why it is important to wear each item in the sun. (to protect their eyes, face, and skin) Children can tell when and where they use sun protection.

 Meeting Individual Needs

Extend Invite children to experiment with sun prints and share their findings. For example, they can leave a sun print in the sun for longer or shorter time periods or try different kinds and colors of paper.

2 Create

Tell children they will do this studio outdoors, where light from the sun will make a print of forms from nature.

Invite children to look at the pictures as you point to and read the steps. You may want to show children an example of a sun print so that they understand what will happen to the paper when it is in the sun.

Technique Tip Some children may want to make a simple scene with the forms, and others may just want to arrange them on the paper in interesting patterns. Encourage either approach.

Quick Studio Children can use fewer objects or share a sheet of construction paper with a partner.

3 Close

Have children use the *Think Like an Artist* question to express ideas about their own work. (Possible response: I used nature to make an artwork.) Encourage children to point out the various colors, forms, and lines in their artworks.

Ongoing Assessment

If . . . children arrange the objects without much thought,

then . . . suggest that they choose objects that will make a pattern across the paper.

See page 72 from **Unit-by-Unit Resources** for a rubric to assess this studio.

Lesson 6

At a Glance

Objectives

- Identify and describe movement in artworks.
- Use drawings that show movement to make a flip book.
- Respond to and make judgments about artworks.

Materials

- sample flip books; crayons; small rectangular books made with stiff paper, stapled so they open horizontally; pencils (optional)
- Rubric 4 from **Unit-by-Unit Resources**

Vocabulary

movement

NVAS (K–4) #1 Understanding and applying media, techniques, and processes

NVAS (K–4) #2 Using knowledge of structures and functions

NVAS (K–4) #3 Choosing and evaluating a range of subject matter, symbols, and ideas

Teach

Ask children to suggest simple movements that they can make sitting down, such as wiggling their fingers or shrugging their shoulders. Use the word *movement* often as everyone performs the exercises.

Display and read page 96 aloud. Discuss what the boys in the drawing and painting are doing. (juggling shells; playing a game.) Help children understand that both artists showed movement by posing the boys' arms and legs as if they were in motion. Ask:

- **How many different movements can you find in the two artworks?** (Possible responses: balls in the air, juggler's arms and hands; boys pushing and pulling, boys running)

Movement

What are the boys doing?

How did the artists show **movement?**

Katsushika Hokusai. *Boy Juggling Shells,* ca. 1800. Ink and color on paper, 13¹¹⁄₁₆ by 9½ inches. The Metropolitan Museum of Art, Charles Stewart Smith, Jr. Collection, gift of Mrs. Charles Stewart Smith, Charles Stewart Smith, Jr., and Howard Caswell Smith, in memory of Charles Stewart Smith, Jr. 1914. [14.76.59(4)]. Photograph © 1996 The Metropolitan Museum of Art.

Winslow Homer. *Snap the Whip,* 1872. Oil on canvas, 22 by 36 inches. Butler Institute of American Art, Youngstown, OH.

96

 Art Background

About the Artist Katsushika Hokusai (1760–1849) used more than 30 different names during his lifetime. The last name he chose was *Gakyo-rojin,* which means "old man mad about painting."

Snap the Whip American painter Winslow Homer (1836–1910) painted realistic scenes of American life, in which children were a favorite subject.

Notes

Lead children in a chant about simple movements they perform: **I can nod, nod, nod my head. I can stretch, stretch, stretch my arms.** Encourage them to join in on the words and the movements.

Make a Flip Book

Studio 6

1 **Draw.**

2 **Move and draw.**

3 **Move and draw.**

4 **Flip.**

Think Like an Artist

How does your book show movement?

97

2 Create

Tell children they will make flip books. Show them the pages in a flip book one at a time to see how the same object is in a slightly different place on each page. Then flip the pages quickly so that children can see the subject "move" inside the book.

Read the steps and then have children watch as you model making a flip book.

Technique Tip Some children may prefer to use a pencil with an eraser to draw the ball on each page. That way, they can draw a few pages, flip them, and redraw whichever pages are not right.

Quick Studio Provide stickers for children to use to model making a flip book.

3 Close

Organize children into small groups to share ideas about their flip books. Remind children to be respectful of others with differing opinions by saying statements such as, **Thank you for your thoughts** or **I will think about that next time.** Then have children answer the *Think Like an Artist* question. (Possible response: The ball looks like it is bouncing.)

Ongoing Assessment

If . . . a child's ball does not seem to move as the book is flipped,

then . . . let him or her try again, this time drawing the balls a little closer together on each page.

See page 72 from **Unit-by-Unit Resources** for a rubric to assess this studio.

 Fine Arts Connection

Music Find orchestral music with radically different tempos, such as a slow lullaby and a very fast piece like "The William Tell Overture" or "Flight of the Bumblebee." Help children recognize the difference in tempos as they listen to both.

 Meeting Individual Needs

Inclusion Some children may not have the fine motor skills needed to flip the pages quickly. Have children draw the picture of the ball on each page and then have another child attach the book together. The partner can flip the pages quickly to show the movement of the ball.

Artist at Work

Artist at Work

Kites

Jose Sainz makes kites. What colors and shapes did he use in this kite?

Jose Sainz

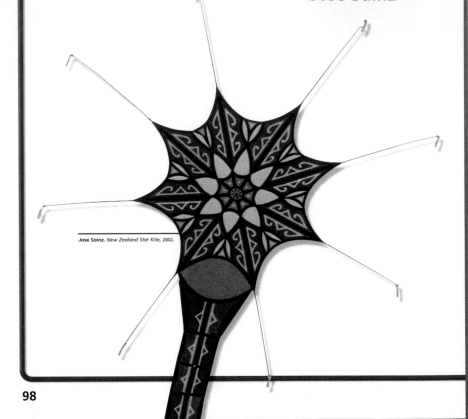

Jose Sainz. *New Zealand Star Kite, 2002.*

98

At a Glance

Objectives

• Read about a career in art.
• Identify the use of art in everyday life.
• Relate art to personal experiences.

Materials

• kite
• Sketchbook Journals

NVAS (K–4) #5 Reflecting upon and assessing the characteristics and merits of their work and the work of others

Explore

Show children a kite and explain how it works. Tell them that a kite is an artwork that is used by many children as a toy in everyday life. Ask children to tell about times they have flown a kite or watched one in the air.

Discuss

Read aloud pages 98 and 99. Tell children that Jose Sainz, the man in the photograph, designed and sewed the kite with the tools shown on page 99. Ask:

• **This kite is twenty feet in diameter! That's almost as big as our room! Why do you think Mr. Sainz made such a huge kite?** (Possible response: so that people on the ground could see it way up in the sky)
• **How is Sainz's kite different from what you see in the store?** (Possible response: It is much bigger and much prettier.)
• **What skills do you need to make a kite?** (Possible responses: you need to be able to sew; use your imagination to create new ideas)

 Career Research

Have children visit the library or look on the Internet to learn more about kites and the people who design and make them. Kite clubs, civic groups, and hobbyists from all over the world have Websites that often include photographs of kite festivals and competitions.

Do the colors and shapes in the kite show balance? How?

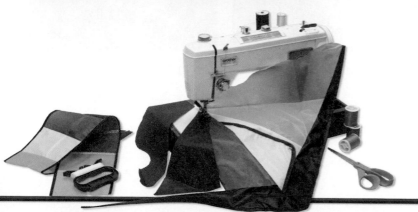

99

Apply

Display a list like the one below. Write the list together as children share their ideas about designing their own kite. Possible responses are shown below.

Designing a Kite
1. Use many colors
2. Use different shapes
3. Make sure the kite has balance
4. Make it fun to look at

Close

Review the completed list and ask: **If you were making a kite, what would it look like?** (Possible response: I would use lots of colors.)

Sketchbook Journal Invite children to draw a kite that they would like to make based on the ideas listed in the chart.

 Reading Strategy

Relate to Personal Experience Remind children that when they read a story, it helps if they know something about the characters or the place where the story happens. Explain that the same is true when they are looking at an artwork.

Ask children to raise their hands if they have flown a kite or watched someone fly one. Invite children to take turns telling one fact about kites or kite-flying that they know from their own experience. Point out how much they already know about the subject.

Portfolio Project

Portfolio Project

At a Glance

Objectives

- Develop and organize ideas from the environment.
- Demonstrate knowledge of weaving and balance.
- Evaluate original artworks by self and peers.

Materials

- pocketbook or pouch, tapestry needles with blunt ends and large eyes ⚠, 16-inch lengths of thin yarn
- 4½- by 9-inch strips of burlap, 1 per child
- sewing scraps, buttons, yarn, sequins or beads
- fabric glue
- feathers (optional)
- Rubric 4 from **Unit-by-Unit Resources**

NVAS (K–4) **#1** Understanding and applying media, techniques, and processes

NVAS (K–4) **#3** Choosing and evaluating a range of subject matter, symbols, and ideas

NVAS (K–4) **#5** Reflecting upon and assessing the characteristics and merits of their work and the work of others

Sew a Pouch

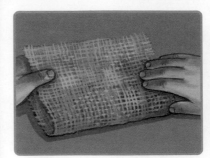
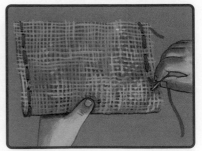

1 Fold.

2 Stitch.

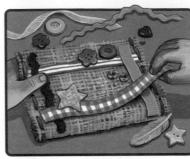
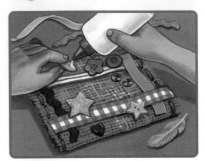

3 Arrange.

4 Glue.

100

Plan

Explain to children that they will create a small pouch, or bag, to hold special objects. Display a small purse or canvas bag and invite children to tell what they might put inside. Display the needle and yarn and ask:

- **This is a needle and yarn. Who can explain how to sew with them?** (Possible response: You poke the needle through some cloth, pull the yarn all the way through, and then do it again.)

Quick Project

Children can make a fabric wall hanging instead of a pouch. They might want to glue colored yarn along the edge as a border.

🚶🚶🚶🚶 Meeting Individual Needs

Reteach Instead of sewing sides of the pouch together, children can staple or glue them shut.

Extend Invite children to choose colored yarn to make a handle or shoulder strap for their pouch. They will have to help each other measure the yarn to make either a shoulder pouch or one that is hand-held.

Look at these pouches.
Children made them.

Rachel, Age 5. *My Purse*. Burlap, buttons, feathers, yarn and sequins.

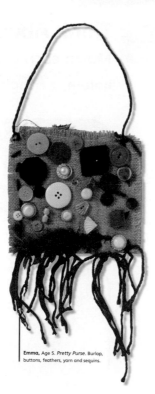

Emma, Age 5. *Pretty Purse*. Burlap, buttons, feathers, yarn and sequins.

Share Your Art

1. Point to details on your pouch.
2. Tell what you will put in your pouch.

 Gallery Options

Show and Tell Treasures Invite children to take their pouches home, choose one object to place inside, and bring the hidden item to school for show and tell. Remind them to ask a family member whether they can bring the item to school.

At sharing time, have children form small groups. Have children share ideas about their peer's artworks. Model by saying: **Shea's pouch shows a variety of lines. I see curved and zigzag lines.**

Then have each child give clues about the treasure inside his or her pouch for classmates to guess. Some children may prefer to simply show the object and tell why they chose it as the special treasure for their pouch.

Create

Gather the materials and guide children through the steps on page 100 to complete the project.

- Remind children to check that the corners meet to make sure the pouch is folded evenly.
- Have children hold the pouch steady with one hand as they sew with the other hand.
- Tell children to choose their design using a variety of colors, forms, and lines. Then encourage them to arrange the objects using balance.
- Remind children to hold each object with a finger as they count to ten to make sure the glue has started to dry.

Children can work on the sewing part of the project at various times over several days. Individuals who are experienced with sewing can help others make neat, uniform stitches along the sides of their pouch.

Close

Point out the children's art on page 101. Ask:

- **Which objects did each artist use?** (buttons, yarn, sequins, and feathers)
- **What makes these pouches unique?** (Answers will vary.)

Use the *Share Your Art* questions to help children express ideas about their own artwork. (Answers will vary.)

See page 72 from **Unit-by-Unit Resources** for a rubric to assess this project.

Unit 4 Review

At a Glance

Objectives

- Relate art terms to the environment.
- Identify forms and balance in artworks.
- Describe, analyze, interpret, and judge an artwork.

Materials

- **Art Print 16**
- children's art portfolios

NVAS (K–4) #1 Understanding and applying media, techniques, and processes

NVAS (K–4) #2 Using knowledge of structures and functions

NVAS (K–4) #5 Reflecting upon and assessing the characteristics and merits of their work and the work of others

Think About Art

Responses:

nature (Point to the landscape.)
balance (Point to the clothing item.)
camera (Point to the camera.)
weaver (Point to the weaver.)

Talk About Art

Prompt children to use words such as *balance, movement,* and *pattern* to describe their artwork. You may also wish to analyze the portfolios for examples of skill development and originality.

Then ask children to choose one artwork from their portfolios to place in a classroom exhibit. Have children walk around the room looking at each other's artworks. Tell them to express ideas about the artworks in the exhibit. Model by saying: **I really like how Keisha created a pattern on her pouch.**

 ### Think About Art

Match each word with a picture.

nature   **balance**   **camera**   **weaver**

 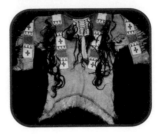

 ### Talk About Art

- Choose one of the artworks you made.
- Tell what makes it special.

102

 ## Assessment Options

Options for assessing children appear in the **Unit-by-Unit Resources.**

- Use the **Vocabulary Worksheets** on pages 65–68 for an informal assessment of Unit 4 vocabulary.
- Use the **Unit 4 Test** on pages 73–76 to assess children's mastery of the unit vocabulary and concepts.

Elizabeth Catlett. *Baile (Dance)*, 1970. Lino-cut, 16 by 30 inches.
© 1996 Elizabeth Catlett/Licensed by VAGA, New York.

Put It All Together

1. What do you see?

2. Point to movement in this print.

3. Why do you think the artist made this print?

4. Who might like this print? Why?

103

Put It All Together

Use the questions on page 103 to evaluate the artwork. Possible responses follow.

1. children dancing; music or singing DESCRIBE

2. The children's gestures suggest movement.
   ANALYZE

3. to show children enjoying themselves by dancing INTERPRET

4. my father, because he loves to dance, too JUDGE

 Art Background

About the Artist Elizabeth Catlett (1915–) is an African American sculptor, printmaker, and painter. The granddaughter of slaves, she has devoted her career to portraying the struggle, courage, and resilience of African American women. Mothers and children are recurring themes in Catlett's art.

Unit 5 Overview

In this unit children will learn about how different artists use many different media to create artworks. The children will also learn to use all of their own senses to explore the different tools and techniques involved in creating artworks.

	Unit Opener, p. 104	Lesson 1, p. 106 **Symbols** **Studio 1, p. 107** Paint a Flag Scene	Lesson 2, p. 108 **Beads** **Studio 2, p. 109** Make a Crown	Lesson 3, p. 110 **Letters** **Studio 3, p. 111** Draw a Letter Picture	Look and Compare, p. 112 **Wood Sculptures**
Artworks	 **Shields Landon Jones.** *Three Musicians,* 1975–1978.		 **Artist unknown,** Yoruba people. *Beaded Crown,* late 19th century.	 **Kjell B. Sandved.** *Butterfly Alphabet Poster,* 1996.	 **Shields Landon Jones.** *Soda Fountain,* 1980s. **Santiago Rozas.** *Qolla Dancers,* ca. 1958.
Vocabulary		symbol	beads	letters	
Materials	• **Art Print 17** • **Instructional Prints**	• red, white, and blue paint; paintbrushes; muffin tins; paint smocks; drawing paper • containers of water and damp paper towels	• beads and a beaded object • scissors ⚠, construction paper, beads and sequins, glue, tape, plastic "jewels" (optional) • tagboard cut in 24"-long strips, approximately three inches wide, one for each child	• alphabet chart • markers, white drawing paper	**Art Prints 17, 18, 19**
Connections	**Home Connection** artworks at home **Bookshelf** *Alphabet Under Construction* by Denise Fleming, Henry Holt, 2002	**Visual Culture** signs and symbols **ESL Notes** **Curriculum Connection** Social Studies: the American flag **Meeting Individual Needs** Extend	**ESL Notes** **Fine Arts Connection** Theatre: pretend to be royalty **Meeting Individual Needs** Inclusion	**ESL Notes** **Technology** Write names **Meeting Individual Needs** Reteach	**Reading Strategy** Identify details
Assessment Opportunities		Rubric 5 from **Unit-by-Unit Resources** Ongoing Assessment	Rubric 5 from **Unit-by-Unit Resources** Ongoing Assessment	Rubric 5 from **Unit-by-Unit Resources** Ongoing Assessment	

Lesson 4, p. 114 **Opposites in Art** **Studio 4, p. 115** **Make Light and Dark Colors**	Lesson 5, p. 116 **Heroes** **Studio 5, p. 117** **Make a Clay Hero**	Lesson 6, p. 118 **Masks** **Studio 6, p. 119** **Make a Paper Mask**	Artist at Work, p. 120 **Playscapes**	Portfolio Project, p. 122 **Make a Jug Mask**	Unit Review, p. 124
Jane Wooster Scott. *Peaceful Harbor,* 1993.	**Selma Burke.** *Martin Luther King, Jr.,* (date not available).	**Artist unknown,** Vuvi people, Gabon. *Mask,* 20th century **Robert Davidson.** *After He Has Seen the Spirit,* 1980	*Black Slide Mantra* by Isamu Noguchi.		**Rhonda Kuhlman and Chris Ake.** *Miss Liberty,* 2002.
	expresses	masks			
• photograph that shows tints and shades of a color • black, white, and blue paint; paintbrushes; muffin tins; paint smocks; drawing paper • containers of water and damp paper towels	• photographs of real-life heroes (optional) • modeling clay, old pencils	• mask • scissors ⚠, construction paper, found objects, glue, craft sticks ⚠	• Sketchbook Journals	• clean, empty gallon milk jugs, one per child • non toxic, all-surface markers • 2-in. squares of tissue paper • diluted glue, large paintbrushes, yarn • found objects • sharp scissors or knife for teacher ⚠	• **Art Print 20** • children's art portfolios
ESL Notes **Curriculum Connection** Math: tints and shades **Meeting Individual Needs** Inclusion	**ESL Notes** **Curriculum Connection** Social Studies: choose a hero **Meeting Individual Needs** Reteach	**ESL Notes** **Fine Arts Connection** Theatre: acting with masks **Meeting Individual Needs** Reteach	**Career Research** People who design outdoor spaces **Reading Strategy** Sequencing	**Gallery Options** Mask dance **Meeting Individual Needs** Extend	
Rubric 5 from **Unit-by-Unit Resources** Ongoing Assessment	Rubric 5 from **Unit-by-Unit Resources** Ongoing Assessment	Rubric 5 from **Unit-by-Unit Resources** Ongoing Assessment		Rubric 5 from **Unit-by-Unit Resources**	**Unit-by-Unit Resources** Vocabulary Worksheets, pp. 83–86 Unit 5 Test, pp. 91–94

Unit 5

At a Glance

Objectives

- Identify the elements of art in artworks.
- Relate art to personal experiences.
- Respond to and make judgments about artworks.

Materials

- **Art Print 17**

NVAS (K–4) #4 Understanding the visual arts in relation to history and cultures

NVAS (K–4) #5 Reflecting upon and assessing the characteristics and merits of their work and the work of others

NVAS (K–4) #6 Making connections between visual arts and other disciplines

Introduce the Unit

Play an audio cassette or CD of familiar children's music. Demonstrate how you can use your sense of hearing to glean information from the environment. Say: **I can hear a banjo in this music,** or **I can hear three people singing.** Ask several volunteers to tell what they hear.

Then display page 104 and invite children's comments about the carvings. Model by expressing your ideas about the carvings. For instance, say: **I like these carvings because they show musicians. I can imagine them playing music that I like.**

Ask children to watch and listen as you recite and perform the finger play "Make Music." Point to each instrument as you pretend to play it. Repeat several times, encouraging children to join in. Then ask:

- **How do you think the musicians feel about their music?** (happy, proud) **How do you know?** (They are all smiling.)

Shields Landon Jones. *Three Musicians*, 1975–1978. Painted wood, tallest figure 43 by 13 by 19 inches. From the collection of Dr. Kurt Gitter and Alice Rae Yelen. © Shields Landon Jones.

 Art Background

Three Musicians In this carved wood grouping by Shields Landon Jones (1901–1997), we are greeted by three smiling country musicians carved from yellow poplar wood and then painted. As is typical of Jones' style, the figures in this artwork stare straight ahead from broad, flat, facial surfaces and have foreshortened torsos.

 Home Connection

Tell children that in this unit, they will learn about artists who liked to explore different ways of making art, such as by carving wood, stringing beads, or using photographs in unusual ways. Encourage children to look for objects at home that are made from a variety of materials and processes. They can share their ideas about them with their classmates.

Artists Explore

Make Music

Pick, pick the banjo,

Strum, strum the guitar.

Play, play the fiddle,

Make music where you are.

Meet the Artist

Shields Landon Jones carves and paints wood to make his sculptures. The tallest musician is almost as tall as you!

105

 Bookshelf

Alphabet Under Construction
by Denise Fleming
Henry Holt, 2002

This alphabet book features a tireless artist mouse that is hard at work constructing letters. In Fleming's colorful pulp paintings, the mouse buttons the *B*, carves the *C*, and so on, until finally, he zips the *Z*. An alphabet poster is included in the back of the book.

Discuss Unit Concepts

Read the title of Unit 5. Tell children that they will use all of their senses to explore and enjoy different ways to make art. Instruct children to look at the artworks in Unit 5. Discuss the different types of artworks and the materials used to make them. Have children talk about artworks that are appealing to them.

Point to the photograph of Shields Landon Jones on page 105 and tell children that he is the artist who created *Three Musicians*. Then read the information about him.

As you talk about the artworks in this unit, you may wish to review the **Instructional Prints.** A print is provided for each element and principle.

Meet the Artist

Shields Landon Jones (1901–1997) Self-taught American folk artist Shields Landon Jones is best known for his portraits in wood. A resident of West Virginia, Jones worked for the railroad and was an accomplished fiddler and banjo player, all common themes in his work. He started carving in his fifties when he was newly retired and widowed, just to keep himself busy. He began with small figures, and then slowly progressed to creating larger ones, including massive portrait heads.

Lesson 1

At a Glance

Objectives

- Identify and describe symbols.
- Use paint to create a scene.
- Respond to and make judgments about artworks.

Materials

- red, white, and blue paint; paintbrushes; muffin tins; paint smocks; drawing paper
- containers of water and damp paper towels
- Rubric 5 from **Unit-by-Unit Resources**

Vocabulary

symbol

NVAS (K–4) #1 Understanding and applying media, techniques, and processes

NVAS (K–4) #2 Using knowledge of structures and functions

NVAS (K–4) #3 Choosing and evaluating a range of subject matter, symbols, and ideas

NVAS (K–4) #6 Making connections between visual arts and other disciplines

1 Teach

Draw a heart, a star, and a stop sign on the board. Invite children to tell what each symbol means to them. (love, good work, stop moving) Tell children that symbols are pictures that have meaning. Symbols most often have the same color and shape each time they are used. For example, a heart is usually red and a star is gold or yellow. Ask children to name the color of the stop sign. (red with white letters) Have children name any other symbols and colors that they recognize.

Read page 106 aloud. Have children find two symbols of our country. (flag, Statue of Liberty) Then ask:

- **Where have you seen these symbols before?** (Possible response: I see the flag in our classroom and the Statue of Liberty on posters.)

Lesson 1

Symbols

Point to the Statue of Liberty.

It is a **symbol** of the United States.

It stands for our country and freedom.

 Visual Culture

Help children compile a scrapbook of visual symbols from their environment, including product logos, traffic signs, and hazard symbols such as the poison label. They can also make their own signs to use in dramatic play activities.

 Notes

Show children useful symbols from everyday life, such as left and right arrows, a skull and crossbones, a litter sign, and so on. Give short commands and model the responses that you expect from children. Say, for example: **Point to POISON. Do not touch! Do not taste!** Repeat the symbol name and then have children say it with you.

Paint a Flag Scene

Studio 1

1. **Think.**

2. **Paint a flag.**

3. **Paint more objects.**

4. **Paint people.**

Art in My World

Name places where you can see the American flag.

107

2 Create

Tell children they will paint the American flag in a landscape, or outdoor picture. Help children brainstorm people and places they might show in their landscape.

As you read the steps, remind children to clean and blot their brush before using a new color. Tell children to include a variety of lines and colors in their paintings.

Technique Tip Tell children that to avoid having paints run into each other, they can paint their flag in stages. Let one color dry before adding another.

Quick Studio Have children paint the American flag in two sessions. Paint the red, white, and blue in session one and the stars in session two.

3 Close

Use the *Art in My World* activity to help children glean information from the environment using their senses.

Ongoing Assessment

If . . . children have trouble painting small details with their paintbrush,

then . . . suggest that they use crayons for the landscape and paint for the flag.

See page 90 from **Unit-by-Unit Resources** for a rubric to assess this studio.

 Curriculum Connection

Social Studies Point to the American flag. Invite a volunteer to tell you what it is and what it means. (It is the American flag and it stands for freedom.) Explain to children that the flag looks different than how it looked when it was first made. Show children a picture of an early American flag. Have children draw a picture of the flag in their Sketchbook Journal.

 Meeting Individual Needs

Extend Have children include personal symbols in their flag scene. If they need help getting started, tell them some of yours. For example, a flower might symbolize your love of gardening.

Lesson 2

At a Glance

Objectives

- Identify and describe artworks made with beads.
- Use a variety of media to make a crown.
- Respond to and make judgments about artworks.

Materials

- beads and a beaded object
- scissors , construction paper, beads and sequins, glue, tape, plastic "jewels" (optional)
- tagboard cut in 24"-long strips, approximately three inches wide, one for each child
- Rubric 5 from **Unit-by-Unit Resources**

Vocabulary

beads

NVAS (K–4) #1 Understanding and applying media, techniques, and processes

NVAS (K–4) #2 Using knowledge of structures and functions

NVAS (K–4) #3 Choosing and evaluating a range of subject matter, symbols, and ideas

NVAS (K–4) #6 Making connections between visual arts and other disciplines

❶ Teach

Display beads and a beaded object. Have children describe the texture and forms of the beads. Show or explain how beads can be sewn or glued to make jewelry or other artworks. Ask children to identify other subjects in the environment that have forms similar to beads. Model by saying: **I have seen forms similar to beads in necklaces and clothing.**

Display and read aloud page 108. Lead children to express ideas about the crown. Have them look closely at the bird. Explain that the artist used the bird as a symbol of power. Ask: **How would you feel if you wore this crown?** (Possible response: important, powerful)

Beads

This artwork is a crown for a king.

It is made of thousands of tiny **beads.**

What is on the very top of the crown?

Artist unknown, Yoruba people. *Beaded Crown,* late 19th century. Basketry, beads, and cloth, 24 by 16½ inches. Brooklyn Museum of Art, New York. Caroline A. L. Pratt Fund, Frederick Loesser Fund, Carl H. De Silva Fund. 70.109.1.

Art Background

Art and Culture This beaded crown was made by the Yoruba people of Nigeria. It would have been part of a royal costume, covered in beads, which denoted the wealth of the ruler. The bird at the top symbolizes power, as does the veil of beads that covers the king's face.

ESL Notes

Display an illustration of a king and a queen. Help children with vocabulary such as *king, queen, robe,* and *crown.* Then lead children in a pantomime of being a king or a queen. For example, pretend to put a crown on your head and say: **I am a queen. I wear a crown on my head.** Encourage children to say whether they are a king or a queen.

Studio 2

Make a Crown

1. **Cut.**
2. **Draw.**
3. **Add beads.**
4. **Tape.**

Think Like an Artist

How is your crown different from your friend's crown?

109

 Fine Arts Connection

Theatre Have children recall stories or movies that include royalty, such as "Cinderella" or "Snow White." Give paper crowns to four volunteers at a time. Help them walk and talk as if they are a king, queen, prince, or princess. Children may want to use the crown they created in the Studio to wear as they dramatize the characters.

 Meeting Individual Needs

Inclusion Children with poor fine-motor coordination will have difficulty grasping and gluing the beads and sequins. Make a paper funnel for them. They can spoon one or two beads at a time into the funnel, positioning the small end over a dab of glue.

② Create

Explain to children that they will make a crown to wear. Invite them to look at the pictures as you point to and read the steps. Demonstrate the process, emphasizing that they can create patterns by arranging the beads or sequins in Step 3. Tell them to add beads and designs that have a variety of colors, forms, and lines.

Technique Tip Show children how to draw the tips of their crown with a pencil first before they cut them out.

Quick Studio Pre-cut the crowns for children to decorate, or have them use markers to draw jewels on their crowns instead of gluing beads.

③ Close

Have children use the *Think Like an Artist* question to express ideas about a peer's artwork. Model with a volunteer. Say: **Jack's crown has a pattern of sequins. My crown has more points and more beads.**

Ongoing Assessment

If . . . children are not happy with how they cut the points of their crown,

then . . . give them another tagboard strip and tell them to draw a line to cut first.

See page 90 from **Unit-by-Unit Resources** for a rubric to assess this studio.

Lesson 3

At a Glance

Objectives

- Identify and describe graphic symbols such as letters in artworks.
- Use markers to make an artwork based on a letter.
- Respond to and make judgments about artworks.

Materials

- alphabet chart
- markers, white drawing paper
- Rubric 5 from **Unit-by-Unit Resources**

Vocabulary

letters

NVAS (K–4) #1 Understanding and applying media, techniques, and processes

NVAS (K–4) #2 Using knowledge of structures and functions

NVAS (K–4) #3 Choosing and evaluating a range of subject matter, symbols, and ideas

NVAS (K–4) #6 Making connections between visual arts and other disciplines

Teach

Display an alphabet chart and invite children to sing the alphabet song. Then lead them in forming letters with their fingers or hands, such as *Cc, Oo, Ll,* and *Vv.*

Display page 110 and read the text aloud. To answer the question, have children look closely to see what each letter is made from. (part of a butterfly wing) Explain that the artist took photographs of lines on butterflies that look like letters and numbers. Identify the different colors on the wings. As you name each color, have children wearing that same color stand and point to the color. Ask:

- **Which letter is the most interesting to you? Why?** (Answers will vary.)

Letters

This poster has rows of **letters.**
It is called *Butterfly Alphabet.*
Why do you think the artist
named it that?

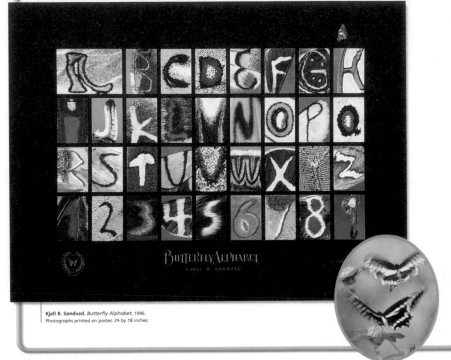

Kjell B. Sandved. *Butterfly Alphabet,* 1996.
Photographs printed on poster, 24 by 18 inches.

Art Background

About the Artist While looking at a moth wing through a microscope one day, Norwegian photographer Kjell Sandved (1922–) found the letter *F*. He then began a search for the rest of the alphabet in the patterns and shapes on insect wings. It would take him to 30 different countries over a period of 25 years!

ESL Notes

Display an alphabet chart. Give children magnetic letters or letter cards. Say each letter name and then have children repeat after you. Model matching a manipulative to a letter on the chart, and have children continue with other letters. As they work, talk about the letter names: **Jonas has a capital *J*. His name starts with *J*.**

Draw a Letter Picture

Studio 3

1. **Choose.**
2. **Write.**
3. **Decorate.**
4. **Share.**

Think Like an Artist

Which letter will you choose next time? Why?

111

 Technology

Write Names Have children experiment with a word processing program. Suggest that they write their name in a standard font. Show them how to change the size and color of the letters, and then have them write their name in different fonts.

 Meeting Individual Needs

Reteach Have children look at their name card before the Studio. Suggest that they choose one of the letters in their name for their letter picture.

2 Create

Explain to children that they will choose a letter from the alphabet and then draw a picture around it, almost as if the letter is "hidden" in the scene.

Invite children to look at the pictures as you point to and read the steps. Ask several volunteers to tell which letter they will use and how they will make it into a picture. Encourage children to use a variety of colors and lines to make sure their letter is hidden.

Technique Tip Model for children how to use the tip of a marker to make thin lines, and the side of the tip to make thicker lines.

Quick Studio Have children draw a picture around the letter *O*. Suggest that they draw an object that is round.

3 Close

Have children use the *Think Like an Artist* questions to reflect on their own work. (Possible response: a *Q*, because it has a tail.)

Ongoing Assessment

If . . . children have trouble writing letters,

then . . . suggest that they choose a letter that is easy to form, such as an *O*, *L*, or *T*.

See page 90 from **Unit-by-Unit Resources** for a rubric to assess this studio.

Look and Compare

Wood Sculptures

What did the artists use
to make these artworks?

How are the sculptures alike?

Shields Landon Jones. *Soda Fountain*, 1980s. Wood, paint, and glass, 16 by 20 by 6 inches. Collection of John and Diane Balsley. Photo: Courtesy Haggerty Museum of Art, Marquette University, Milwaukee, WI.

112

At a Glance

Objectives

- Compare and contrast two artworks.
- Respond to and make judgments about artworks.

Materials

- Art Prints 17, 18, 19

NVAS (K–4) #4 Understanding the visual arts in relation to history and cultures

NVAS (K–4) #5 Reflecting upon and assessing the characteristics and merits of their work and the work of others

Explore

Display **Art Print 17,** *Three Musicians*. Help children recall this sculpture by Shields Landon Jones from page 104. As children look at the two artworks on pages 112–113, invite them to predict which one was also created by Jones and give reasons for their answer. (*Soda Fountain*; The people have the same large faces.) Have children share ideas about the two sculptures by Jones. Model by saying that both sculptures have similar looking people and that each sculpture is made with the same materials. Remind children to show respect for their classmates who may have differing opinions.

Discuss

Read pages 112–113 aloud. Have children identify the simple subject of each sculpture. (people at a soda fountain, three dancers) Talk about how each sculpture features people, however the people are performing different actions.

Then ask children to name the material that both sculptors used. (wood) Lead children to talk about what they might hear in each sculpture. (people slurping from straws; music)

 Art Background

Art and Culture *Soda Fountain* is an example of the folk art from the Appalachian region of America. Many of these artists are self-taught, and whittling or carving wood is a popular way of making artworks. Folk artists often create art that directly reflects their lives, environment, and values.

Qolla Dancers These small but highly detailed sculptures are carved from cactus wood and then painted. During the festival at Paucartambo in Peru, men dress as *qollas*, or ancient traders. These are the two figures on either end. Emilia, the shepherdess, is in the middle. At the festival, she is played by a boy.

Santiago Rozas. *Qolla Dancers*, ca. 1958. Painted cactus wood. Girard Collection. Museum of International Folk Art, Santa Fe, NM. Photo by Michel Monteaux.

Which sculpture would you like
to be in?

Explain why.

Tell what you might hear in each.

113

Reading Strategy

Identify Details Tell children that when they read a story or look at an artwork, they should think about the small parts, or details. Create a folk art exhibit in your classroom. Ask parents to send in examples of folk art from their homes for a "Look Only" exhibit.

Have children identify details about each artwork. Then ask them to express ideas about the folk art in the exhibition. Model by saying: **Each artwork in this exhibition is made by a different artist. Each artwork is original. Some artworks are useful.**

Apply

Draw a Venn diagram like the one below on the chalkboard. Tell children that this graphic organizer is a good way to show how two artworks are the same and different.

To fill in the diagram, suggest that children first compare the artworks, looking for ways they are alike. Fill in the middle section as children suggest ideas. Guide children as they look for differences by suggesting that they focus on the subjects of the two artworks. Possible responses are shown in blue.

Wood Sculptures

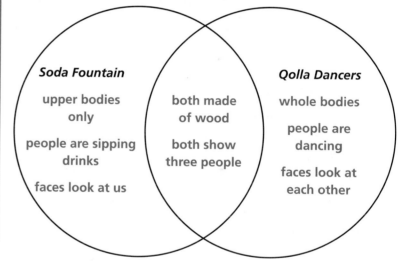

Soda Fountain

upper bodies only

people are sipping drinks

faces look at us

both made of wood

both show three people

Qolla Dancers

whole bodies

people are dancing

faces look at each other

Close

Ask children what they learned about sculptures that show people. (Possible response: An artist can choose how much of a person's body to show and what actions to show.)

Lesson 4

At a Glance

Objectives

- Identify and describe opposites in an artwork.
- Mix tints and shades of blue paint.
- Respond to and make judgments about artworks.

Materials

- photograph that shows tints and shades of a color
- black, white, and blue paint; paintbrushes; muffin tins; paint smocks; drawing paper
- containers of water and damp paper towels
- Rubric 5 from **Unit-by-Unit Resources**

NVAS (K–4) #1 Understanding and applying media, techniques, and processes

NVAS (K–4) #2 Using knowledge of structures and functions

Teach

Share with children a photograph that has many objects that have the same color, such as a field of blue flowers, or a basket of blueberries. Ask children to name the colors they see. Explain that even though all of the objects are blue, some are light blue and others are darker.

Tell children the lighter versions of a color are called *tints* and the darker versions of a color are called *shades*. Light and dark tints and shades are opposites. Point out other examples of tints and shades in the environment. Name a color and have children look for and identify tints and shades of that color in the classroom.

Then have children express ideas about Jane Wooster Scott's painting. Model by saying: **The tints and shades of blue in the water make it look realistic.**

Opposites in Art

Look for opposites.

Find light blue and dark blue.

What is close?

What is far away?

Jane Wooster Scott. *Peaceful Harbor,* 1993. Oil on canvas.

114

 Art Background

About the Artist American folk painter Jane Wooster Scott is listed in the *Guinness Book of Records* as one of the most reproduced artists in America. Noted for her paintings of Americana, she depicts holidays, celebrations, and traditions in great detail.

ESL Notes

Display sets of paint chips that show shades and tints of various colors. Invite children to sequence three or more hues of a color from lightest to darkest. Then ask questions such as: **Is this blue or orange? Is this light blue or dark blue?**

Studio 4

Make Light and Dark Colors

① Mix.

② Clean.

③ Mix.

④ Paint.

Think Like an Artist

What did you learn about light and dark colors?

115

 Curriculum Connection

Math Organize children into pairs. Have each pair name a color. From a box of 64 crayons, ask them to remove all the tints and shades of their color. Then have them count the number of crayons they removed. Have pairs share their color and number with the class and determine which color has the most tints and shades in the crayon box.

 Meeting Individual Needs

Inclusion Some children who are visually impaired may not be able to distinguish among the tints and shades of a color, but will still enjoy mixing paints and painting a picture.

② Create

Tell children they will mix a tint and a shade of blue, using white, blue, and black paints. Then point to and read the steps. Explain that in Step 1, they must put small dabs of blue into the white.

Technique Tip Tell children to add very small amounts of black to the blue in Step 3, and mix the paint thoroughly after each addition. Just small amounts of black will darken another color very quickly.

⏱ Quick Studio Organize children into pairs. Have one child mix a tint of a color and the other child mix a shade of the same color. Then have pairs share them to paint pictures.

③ Close

Have children use the *Think Like an Artist* question to reflect on their own work. (Possible response: I learned how to use white and black to make other blues.)

Continue to look at examples of tints and shades by having children look at Jane Wooster Scott's portfolio. Provide a portfolio, or a book, of Scott's artworks. Ask children to point out tints and shades. Then have them express ideas. Model by saying: **Scott's paintings are colorful.**

Ongoing Assessment

If . . . children add too much black to the blue,

then . . . let them start over, adding a very small amount of black into the blue paint.

See page 90 from **Unit-by-Unit Resources** for a rubric to assess this studio.

Lesson 5

At a Glance

Objectives

- Identify and describe feelings expressed in artworks.
- Use clay to make a sculpture of a hero.
- Respond to and make judgments about artworks.

Materials

- photographs of real-life heroes (optional)
- modeling clay, old pencils
- Rubric 5 from **Unit-by-Unit Resources**

Vocabulary

expresses

NVAS (K–4) #1 Understanding and applying media, techniques, and processes

NVAS (K–4) #2 Using knowledge of structures and functions

NVAS (K–4) #3 Choosing and evaluating a range of subject matter, symbols, and ideas

Teach

Explain to children that a hero is a person who has done something special to help other people. Share pictures of heroes, such as Susan B. Anthony, Abraham Lincoln, and Sojourner Truth. Talk about why these people are considered heroes.

Then ask children to name some heroes they know. Prompt them with categories such as community helpers, athletes, friends, and family. Discuss what makes each person a hero.

Display and read page 116. Discuss the statue and name its subject. (Dr. Martin Luther King, Jr.) Then share your ideas on the statue. For instance, say: **This is an important statue to me because the subject, Dr. Martin Luther King, Jr., is a hero. The artist made this statue so realistic that it looks just like the man.** Ask children to share ideas and feelings about the statue.

Heroes

Who is a hero to you? Why?
This sculpture **expresses** feelings about a hero.

Selma Burke. *Martin Luther King, Jr.*, 1980. Bronze, height approximately 20 feet. Charlotte, NC.

116

 Art Background

About the Artist African American sculptor Selma Burke (1900–1995) created the portrait of Franklin Delano Roosevelt that was used for his profile on the United States dime. She was the founder of the Selma Burke School of Sculpture in New York and the Selma Burke Art Center in Pittsburgh.

ESL **Notes**

Collect several pictures of American heroes. Invite a volunteer to choose a picture. Name the person in the picture. Say: **This is Thomas Jefferson. He is a hero.** Then have children repeat after you. Explain to children why this person is considered a hero. Then, continue by asking each child to choose a different picture.

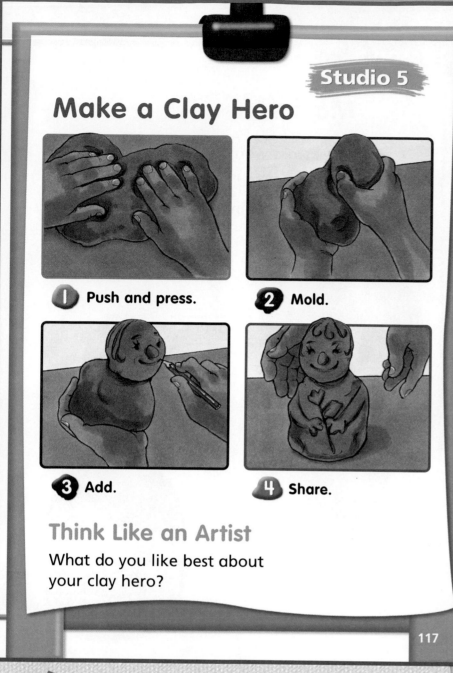

Make a Clay Hero

Studio 5

1. **Push and press.**
2. **Mold.**
3. **Add.**
4. **Share.**

Think Like an Artist

What do you like best about your clay hero?

117

 Curriculum Connection

Social Studies Help children choose someone who is a hero to them. It might be a famous person, a school or community helper, or a family member. Have children complete this sentence about the person: _____ **is a hero because** _____. Ask them: **What might a sculpture of** _____ **show?**

 Meeting Individual Needs

Reteach For children who have a hard time choosing a hero to create, remind them that family members and friends are often heroes. Encourage them to create a sculpture of someone special to them.

② Create

Tell children they will mold, or make, a hero from clay. Display photographs of heroes. Help children identify the subject of each photograph. Invite them to brainstorm ideas by choosing a hero from the photographs. Children may also want to choose people in their community, at school, or in their family for whom they would like to create a statue.

Invite children to look at the steps as you explain them. Review how to pinch and pull body parts or roll arms and legs and attach them to the torso.

Technique Tip Tell children they can use clothing or a prop to identify their hero. For example, they might show an athlete holding a clay ball.

Quick Studio Children can make a clay bust, or just the head and neck, of their hero.

③ Close

Create your own clay hero to model expressing ideas about a personal artwork. Then have children use the *Think Like an Artist* question to express ideas about their own work. (Possible response: I like how my hero looks like she is smiling.)

Ongoing Assessment

If . . . children have trouble adding details with a pencil,

then . . . suggest that they roll or mold smaller pieces of clay and add them to their figures as clothing, facial features, or a prop.

See page 90 from **Unit-by-Unit Resources** for a rubric to assess this studio.

Lesson 6

At a Glance

Objectives

- Identify and describe masks.
- Use scissors and found objects to make a mask.
- Respond to and make judgments about artworks.

Materials

- mask
- scissors ⚠, construction paper, found objects, glue, craft sticks ⚠
- Rubric 5 from **Unit-by-Unit Resources**

Vocabulary

masks

NVAS (K–4) #1 Understanding and applying media, techniques, and processes

NVAS (K–4) #2 Using knowledge of structures and functions

NVAS (K–4) #3 Choosing and evaluating a range of subject matter, symbols, and ideas

NVAS (K–4) #6 Making connections between visual arts and other disciplines

---

Lesson 6

Masks

Masks are worn over your face. Masks express different feelings. Why do you think people made these masks?

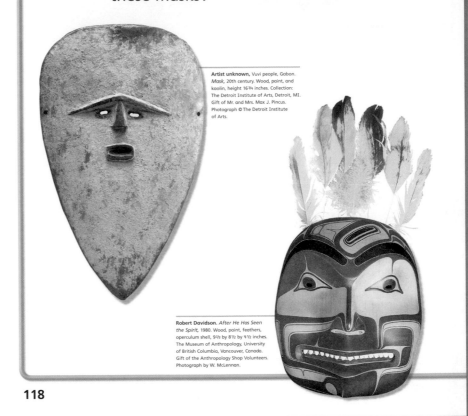

Artist unknown, Vuvi people, Gabon. *Mask,* 20th century. Wood, paint, and kaolin, height 16¾ inches. Collection: The Detroit Institute of Arts, Detroit, MI. Gift of Mr. and Mrs. Max J. Pincus. Photograph © The Detroit Institute of Arts.

Robert Davidson. *After He Has Seen the Spirit,* 1980. Wood, paint, feathers, operculum shell, 9²⁄₃ by 8½ by 4½ inches. The Museum of Anthropology, University of British Columbia, Vancouver, Canada. Gift of the Anthropology Shop Volunteers. Photograph by W. McLennan.

118

---

① Teach

Display a mask and describe the colors, form, and textures. Invite volunteers to tell about a time they wore a mask. Ask: **Did it have many colors? Describe its form. Did it have texture? How did you feel when you were wearing the mask?**

Display and read page 118. Point out that the Vuvi mask is only one color, while Davidson's mask has many colors and lines. Have children express other ideas about the masks. Ask: **Which of these masks would you like to wear? Why?** (Possible response: the one on the right because it has feathers and bright colors)

Art Background

Art History Masks have been worn by people for centuries. The tradition and art of mask-making is found all over the world. People from different cultures wear masks to disguise themselves and for protection.

ESL Notes

Let children take turns wearing a simple mask over their eyes, or display several masks that imply different feelings, such as sad, scary, silly, and so on. Point out features of the masks in simple sentences and encourage children to tell how they might feel wearing each one.

Studio 6

Make a Paper Mask

1 Fold.

2 Draw. Cut.

3 Glue.

4 Hold.

Think Like an Artist

How does the mask make you feel? Why?

119

See page 90 from **Unit-by-Unit Resources** for a rubric to assess this studio.

Fine Arts Connection

Theatre Tell children that in many cultures, people wear masks when they perform a play. Invite them to act out a familiar story, such as "The Three Billy Goats Gruff." Encourage the actors to make a mask for their character, or provide simple masks. Have children in the audience tell whether the masks added to their enjoyment of the play.

Meeting Individual Needs

Reteach Display a mask and show children how it is exactly the same on both sides of the nose. Fold children's paper and draw eyeholes and a mouth in advance for them to cut out.

2 Create

Tell children they will fold, cut, and decorate construction paper with fun shapes and forms to make their own mask. Discuss the variety of colors, forms, and lines children can use to create a mask.

Then have children follow along as you read the steps. During Step 2, children may need help to draw the lines on the fold for the eyes, nose, and mouth.

Technique Tip Some children may prefer to cut the eyeholes and mouth without folding the paper. Help them to measure and mark where they should cut.

Quick Studio Have precut white paper plates for children to decorate with markers or crayons.

3 Close

Create your own mask to model expressing ideas about a personal artwork. Then have children use the *Think Like an Artist* questions to express ideas about their own work. (Possible response: I feel like a fierce lion behind my mask.)

Ongoing Assessment

If . . . children have trouble looking out of the eyeholes of their mask,

then . . . help them cut tiny amounts of paper out of each eyehole until they can see comfortably through them.

Artist at Work

Explore

Tell children that many playgrounds are considered artworks because they show the elements of art. Ask children to visualize the playground at their school or a favorite one in their community. Invite several volunteers to describe the colors, lines, and forms found in the playground. Ask: **What is your favorite playground equipment? Describe it.** (Possible response: I like the slide. It is a triangular form.)

Discuss

Explain that playscapes are artworks that children use in everyday life. Read aloud pages 120–121. Tell children that Isamu Noguchi, the man in the photograph, planned the playscape shown. Ask:

- **How is this playscape different from playgrounds you have used in everyday life?** (Possible response: The slide looks like an artwork.)
- **Would you like to play on this playscape? Why or why not?** (Possible response: Yes; I like how the play places look like sculptures.)
- **What skills do you need to create a playscape?** (Possible responses: You need to know about forms and how to arrange them. You need to know how to do landscape design.)

Playscapes

Isamu Noguchi used simple forms.

He created gardens and parks.

His parks are artworks.

Children love to play on his playscapes.

Isamu Noguchi

 Career Research

Take children on a walk to visit a playground, park, or garden. As you walk around the space together, point out features that the designer included to make the place more inviting or functional. Ask them to suggest why he or she put benches in a particular place, why there is a fence around the perimeter, and so on.

Isamu Noguchi.
Black Slide Mantra,
installed 1992.
Black granite.

Imagine you are in this park.

What would you like to explore?

A Noguchi playscape in Atlanta, GA

121

 Reading Strategy

Sequencing Remind children that when they read a story, it helps to think about what happens first, next, and last. Explain that the same is true when they are looking at an artwork.

Ask each child to imagine he or she is Isamu Noguchi, looking at an empty field where he or she will build a playscape. Help children brainstorm what they would need to do first, and list all reasonable ideas. Then talk about what would have to happen next and last. Choose three or four ideas that show the best sequence and write a short paragraph together about creating a playscape.

Apply

Display a graphic organizer like the one below. Fill in the boxes together as children share their ideas about the sequence of events in building a playscape. Possible responses are shown below.

Building a Playscape

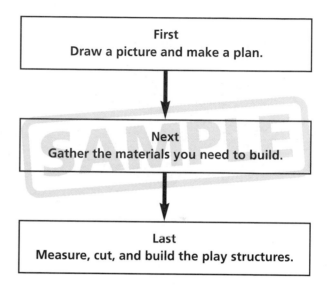

Close

Review the completed diagram and ask: **What if you forgot to make a plan first?** (Possible response: The play structures might be too big for the space.)

Sketchbook Journal Invite children to draw a playground or piece of equipment that they would like to play in or on.

Portfolio Project

Portfolio Project

At a Glance

Objectives

- Develop and organize ideas from the environment.
- Use found objects to make a jug mask.
- Evaluate original artworks by self and peers.

Materials

- clean, empty gallon milk jugs, one per child
- non-toxic all-surface markers
- 2-in. squares of tissue paper
- diluted glue, large paintbrushes, yarn
- found objects
- sharp scissors or knife for teacher ⚠ⓢ
- Rubric 5 from **Unit-by-Unit Resources**

NVAS (K–4) #1 Understanding and applying media, techniques, and processes

NVAS (K–4) #5 Reflecting upon and assessing the characteristics and merits of their work and the work of others

Make a Jug Mask

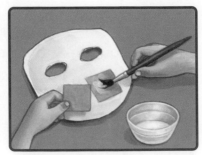

1 Mark.   **2** Glue.

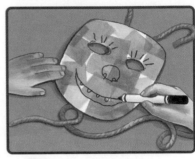

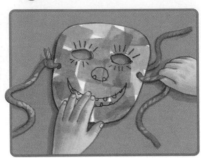

3 Decorate.   **4** Tie.

122

Plan

In advance, cut and throw away the back of each jug. Punch a hole in the sides so that children can thread string or yarn through the holes.

Explain to children that they will make masks from milk jugs. Display the masks on page 118 and review the features of a mask. (eyeholes, a mouth, a way to hold it against your face) Ask:

- **How can you use yarn to decorate your mask?**
- **What colors will you use to create your mask?**
- **What mood do you want your mask to express?**

Quick Project

Use 8-by-12-inch pieces of cardboard instead of jugs and slightly bend the cardboard in the middle for a better fit.

👪 Meeting Individual Needs

Extend Children can dip various lengths of yarn into diluted glue and lay them on paper towels in interesting lines and shapes, such as zigzags or coils. When the yarn is dry, children can attach one end of each stiffened shape on the jug to be silly hair.

How do these masks make you feel?

Cassie, Age 6. *Button Mouth.* Plastic jug, colored tissue, cotton balls, yarn, buttons.

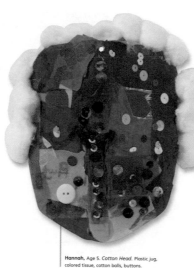

Hannah, Age 5. *Cotton Head.* Plastic jug, colored tissue, cotton balls, buttons.

Share Your Art

1. Tell about the face on your mask.

2. Where will you wear your mask?

123

Gallery Options

Mask Dance Show photographs or a short video of people dancing with masks. Talk about the masks, why the people are wearing them, and what the dance means culturally.

Teach children a simple circle or line dance that they can perform in small groups. Have them practice the steps without masks first. Then invite small groups to take turns performing the dance with their masks. Afterward, ask volunteers to tell how they felt when they danced behind their masks.

Create

Gather the materials and guide children through the steps on page 122 to complete the project. Remind children to create their masks using a variety of colors, forms, and lines.

• In Step 1, check children's marks before cutting into the jug with scissors or a knife.
• Model with children how they should glue after they arrange the tissue paper and the found objects into an orderly arrangement.
• Remind children that they can draw whatever kind of mouth they want such as talking, smiling, funny, and so on.
• For Step 4, help children tie the masks on their heads.

Close

Point out the children's art on page 123. Ask:

• **What feelings does each mask express?** (Possible response: The bright colors make the masks seem happy.)

Create your own mask and model sharing ideas about it. Say: **I like how my mask turned out because it looks just like a bear. I feel strong when I wear it.** Then have small groups answer the *Share Your Art* questions as they share ideas about their own artwork and the artworks of others. Remind children to be respectful of classmates with differing opinions by prompting them to use phrases such as, **Thanks for your ideas** and **I'll keep that in mind for my next artwork.**

See page 90 from **Unit-by-Unit Resources** for a rubric to assess this project.

Unit 5 Review

At a Glance

Objectives

- Relate art terms to the environment.
- Identify symbols in artworks.
- Describe, analyze, interpret, and judge artworks.

Materials

- **Art Print 20**
- children's art portfolios

NVAS (K–4) #1 Understanding and applying media, techniques, and processes

NVAS (K–4) #2 Using knowledge of structures and functions

NVAS (K–4) #5 Reflecting upon and assessing the characteristics and merits of their work and the work of others

Think About Art

Possible responses:

beads (Point to the beads.)
playscape (Point to the playground.)
symbol (Point to the flag, stop sign, and heart.)
mask (Point to the mask.)

Talk About Art

Have children name their favorite subject to use in an artwork. Say, for instance, **I like to create artworks about nature.** Then ask children to choose an artwork from their portfolios that demonstrates this subject and describe it.

Prompt children to use words such as *express* and *symbol* to describe their artwork. Children may also wish to express ideas about the portfolios of peers. Encourage them to identify the subject in each artwork. Model by saying: **I like Mark's painting. The subject is a bird.**

Unit Review

 Think About Art

Match each word with a picture.

beads   playscape   symbols   mask

 Talk About Art

- Share one of your artworks.
- Tell what makes it special.
- Who would like it most? Why?

124

 Assessment Options

Options for assessing children appear in the **Unit-by-Unit Resources.**

- Use the **Vocabulary Worksheets** on pages 83–86 for an informal assessment of Unit 5 vocabulary.
- Use the **Unit 5 Test** on pages 91–94 to assess children's mastery of unit vocabulary and concepts.

Put It All Together

1. What do you see?

2. How did the artists put it together?

3. Why do you think the artists used this symbol of America?

4. How do you feel when you look at this sculpture?

Rhonda Kuhlman and Chris Ake. *Miss Liberty,* 2002.
Recycled bottle caps, tin, and wood, 18 by 33 by 2½ inches.
RC Gallery and Recycled Works. San Antonio, TX.

125

Put It All Together

Use the questions on page 125 to evaluate the artwork. Possible responses follow.

1. a Statue of Liberty made from bottle caps DESCRIBE

2. by gluing bottle caps to a sculpture of the Statue of Liberty ANALYZE

3. because they wanted to use found items that originate in the United States. INTERPRET

4. amused, proud JUDGE

 Art Background

Art History The Statue of Liberty, one of the most recognizable symbols of America, has been the inspiration of many artists, each with his or her own vision of Lady Liberty. She has appeared in everything from neon sculptures to weather vanes, and has been modeled in every conceivable material, from bottle caps to papier-mâché.

Unit 6 Overview

Artists tell stories through their artwork. They might use buildings, murals, or show people at play to tell their stories. In this unit, children will learn different ways to tell stories through art. They will create their own artworks using the elements of art and principles of design.

	Unit Opener, p. 126	Lesson 1, p. 128 **Buildings** Studio 1, p. 129 **Draw a Building**	Lesson 2, p. 130 **Spaces at Home** Studio 2, p. 131 **Draw an Indoor Space**	Lesson 3, p. 132 **Furniture** Studio 3, p. 133 **Make Wire Furniture**	Look and Compare, p. 134 **Art That Tells a Story**
Artworks	 **John Biggers.** *Starry Crown*, 1987.		 **Horace Pippin.** *Victorian Parlor II*, 1945.	 **Michael Moss.** *Rocking Chair*, 1993.	 **John Biggers.** *Jubilee*, date unknown. **Attributed to Bihzad.** *Building of the Palace of Khawarnaq*, ca. 1494.
Vocabulary		architects	indoor spaces, outdoor spaces	furniture	
Materials	• **Art Print 21** • **Instructional Prints**	• drawing paper, pencils, crayons	• decorating magazines or catalogs • markers, pencils, drawing paper	• pipe cleaners ⚠, construction paper scraps, shoe boxes or other display materials	**Art Prints 21, 22, 23**
Connections	**Home Connection** visual stories **Bookshelf** *Who's in Rabbit's House?:* retold by Verna Aardema, Dial, 1969	**Visual Culture** compare and contrast buildings **ESL Notes** **Curriculum Connection** Math: counting materials **Meeting Individual Needs** Reteach	**ESL Notes** **Fine Arts Connection** Dance: space movements **Meeting Individual Needs** Inclusion	**ESL Notes** **Curriculum Connection** Math: graphs, charts, and illustrated lists **Meeting Individual Needs** Reteach	**Reading Strategy** Draw conclusions
Assessment Opportunities		Rubric 6 from **Unit-by-Unit Resources** Ongoing Assessment	Rubric 6 from **Unit-by-Unit Resources** Ongoing Assessment	Rubric 6 from **Unit-by-Unit Resources** Ongoing Assessment	

Lesson 4, p. 136 Murals **Studio 4, p. 137** Make a Mural	Lesson 5, p. 138 Games **Studio 5, p. 139** Draw a Game	Lesson 6, p. 140 People at Play **Studio 6, p. 141** Make a Crayon Resist	Artist at Work, p. 142 **Folded Paper**	Portfolio Project, p. 144 **Weave a Fence**	Unit Review, p. 146
 Diego Rivera. *Surface Miners,* 1923.	 **Artist unknown.** *A Lion and Antelope Play Senet,* 1250–1150 B.C.	 **Paul Gauguin.** *Breton Girls Dancing, Pont-Aven,* 1888.	 *origami birds* by Jodi Fukumoto.		 **Natalia Goncharova.** *The Harvest,* ca.1909.
murals		contrast	origami		
• tape, butcher paper, crayons or markers	• photographs of people playing indoor and outdoor games (optional) • drawing paper, pencils, crayons	• dark-color crayons, drawing paper, wide paintbrushes, diluted light-color tempera paint	• origami (optional) • Sketchbook Journals	• chain-link fence or indoor loom • fabric scraps cut in long strips • ribbons, crêpe paper, yarn, twine • long grass stems	• **Art Print 24** • children's art portfolios
ESL Notes **Curriculum Connection** Health: mural of health topics **Meeting Individual Needs** Inclusion	**ESL Notes** **Curriculum Connection** Social Studies: memory game **Meeting Individual Needs** Extend	**ESL Notes** **Fine Arts Connection** Music: musicians and composers use contrast **Meeting Individual Needs** Inclusion	**Career Research** People who work with their hands **Reading Strategy** Identify cause and effect relationships	**Meeting Individual Needs** Extend, Inclusion **Gallery Options** Weaving exhibition	
Rubric 6 from **Unit-by-Unit Resources** Ongoing Assessment	Rubric 6 from **Unit-by-Unit Resources** Ongoing Assessment	Rubric 6 from **Unit-by-Unit Resources** Ongoing Assessment		Rubric 6 from **Unit-by-Unit Resources**	**Unit-by-Unit Resources** Vocabulary Worksheets, pp. 101–104 Unit 6 Test, pp. 109–112

Unit 6

At a Glance

Objectives

- Identify cultural expression in artworks.
- Relate art to personal experiences.
- Respond to and make judgments about artworks.

Materials

- Art Print 21

NVAS (K–4) #4 Understanding the visual arts in relation to history and cultures

NVAS (K–4) #5 Reflecting upon and assessing the characteristics and merits of their work and the work of others

NVAS (K–4) #6 Making connections between visual arts and other disciplines

Introduce the Unit

Describe the job of a storyteller. Explain that storytellers tell stories in very interesting ways. They may use different voices, props, or puppets to help them tell stories. Ask several volunteers to tell about storytellers they have heard at the library or seen on television. Then display page 126 and explain that the three women in the painting are storytellers.

Ask children to watch and listen as you recite and act out "Starry Crown." Hold up three fingers, pretend to read a book, and take a bow as you say the rhyme. Repeat several times, encouraging children to join in. Then ask:

- **The name of this painting is *Starry Crown.* Why do you think the artist chose that title?** (Possible response: because the women look like they are wearing crowns)
- **Do you like this painting? Why?** (Possible response: Yes, I like the three storyteller's robes. They look like they are for special occasions.)

John Biggers. *Starry Crown,* 1987. Acrylic on canvas, 59½ by 47½ inches. Dallas Museum of Art, Dallas, TX.

126

 Art Background

Starry Crown The title of this painting comes from a line in an African American spiritual. The three women are dressed in the costumes of the Beninese, Egyptian, and Dogon cultures of Africa. The center figure is making a star shape with string, symbolizing the importance of storytelling. The quilt in the painting is a symbol of women's creativity.

 Home Connection

Tell children that in this unit, they will learn about artists who tell visual stories, or stories you can see. Encourage children to look through picture books at home to discover how other storytellers used pictures or photographs to tell a visual story.

Visual Stories

Starry Crown

Three storytellers,

Will you tell a story now?

And when you are finished,

Please take a bow.

Meet the Artist

John Biggers was an art teacher and an artist. Many of his artworks use symbols and shapes from Africa.

 Bookshelf

Who's in Rabbit's House?
retold by Verna Aardema
Dial, 1969

This rhythmic read-aloud is a retelling of a classic Masai tale about a rabbit with a problem. Leo Dillon, one of the illustrators, was the first African American artist to win a Caldecott medal.

Discuss Unit Concepts

Read the title of Unit 6. Tell children that they will learn how artists tell stories through their artworks. Point to the photograph of John Biggers on page 127 and tell children that he is the artist who painted *Starry Crown.* Then read the information about him.

As you talk about the artworks in this unit, you may wish to review the **Instructional Prints.** A print is provided for each element and principle taught in kindergarten.

Meet the Artist

African American artist John Biggers (1924–2001) studied art at Hampton Institute in Virginia, where a teacher encouraged him to explore his African heritage. Biggers went on to become the founding chairman of the art department at Texas Southern University. He initiated a mural program there in which every senior student who was an art major was expected to complete a mural on campus.

In 1957 Biggers traveled to Africa on a study tour of African traditions and culture. After the trip, he began to include recurring symbols based on African art and folklore in his paintings.

Lesson 1

At a Glance

Objectives

- Identify and describe architects.
- Plan and draw a building.
- Respond to and make judgments about artworks.

Materials

- drawing paper, pencils, crayons
- Rubric 6 from **Unit-by-Unit Resources**

Vocabulary

architects

NVAS (K–4) #1 Understanding and applying media, techniques, and processes

NVAS (K–4) #2 Using knowledge of structures and functions

NVAS (K–4) #3 Choosing and evaluating a range of subject matter, symbols, and ideas

NVAS (K–4) #6 Making connections between visual arts and other disciplines

Teach

Take a short walk around school. Ask children to point out the colors, textures, and forms of the school buildings. Invite children to identify features of the school building(s), such as the roof, the walls, and the doors, and discuss the purposes for each. Tell children that an architect planned what forms to use to create their school building.

Ask children whether they would like to visit the museum in the photograph. Then read page 128 aloud. Ask:

- **What is the first thing you noticed on this building?** (the sculptures that look like children)
- **How would you feel inside this building? Why?** (excited; It looks like an adventure is ahead.)

Lesson 1

Buildings

Architects plan buildings.
They think about how a building
should look and then draw it.
An architect planned this museum.

Nek Chand. *Fantasy Sculpture Garden,* 1985. Capitol Children's Museum, Washington, D.C.

128

 Visual Culture

Help children compile a list of buildings in their neighborhood. Choose two that most children know, such as a fire station and your school. Invite children to tell how the buildings are the same and how they are different. For example, most of a fire station is a garage for fire trucks; most of a school is classrooms for children.

ESL Notes

Let children build a building using various materials. Encourage them to describe what they are doing, helping them with vocabulary such as *roof, wall,* and *door.* Ask questions about the buildings: **Is this a wall or a roof? What color is the door? Whose building is tallest?**

Draw a Building

1 **Think.**

2 **Draw.**

3 **Add.**

4 **Color.**

Art in My World

Draw your favorite building in your community.

129

 Curriculum Connection

Math In advance, prepare building "kits." Place identical building materials in three different shoe boxes. Give each kit to a child. Explain that children will have five minutes to build a building using as many of the items in their kit as they can. When time is up, have each child discuss their building. Ask children to count how many items they used to build their building. Then have children sketch their buildings in their Sketchbook Journal.

 Meeting Individual Needs

Reteach In preparation for the Studio, display photographs of several buildings. Invite children to choose one to describe, telling about its roof, walls, windows, and doors. Have them decide what the building is probably used for and how they know.

2 Create

Tell children they will plan and draw a building using a variety of colors and lines. Help children brainstorm real and imaginary buildings they might like to draw.

As you read the steps in the Studio, remind children to use most of their paper so that their building is big enough to add details such as windows and doors.

Technique Tip To blend colors with crayons, tell children to color with the lighter color first, and then gently color over it with the darker color.

Quick Studio Have children draw a home they would like to live in.

3 Close

Use the *Art in My World* activity to help children glean information from the environment, using their senses.

Ongoing Assessment

If . . . children have trouble thinking of a building to draw,

then . . . suggest that they draw their home or school.

See page 108 from **Unit-by-Unit Resources** for a rubric to assess this studio.

Lesson 2

At a Glance

Objectives

- Identify and describe indoor and outdoor spaces.
- Use markers and crayons to draw an indoor space.
- Respond to and make judgments about artworks.

Materials

- decorating magazines or catalogs
- markers, pencils, drawing paper
- Rubric 6 from **Unit-by-Unit Resources**

Vocabulary

indoor spaces, outdoor spaces

NVAS (K–4) #1 Understanding and applying media, techniques, and processes

NVAS (K–4) #2 Using knowledge of structures and functions

NVAS (K–4) #3 Choosing and evaluating a range of subject matter, symbols, and ideas

NVAS (K–4) #6 Making connections between visual arts and other disciplines

---

Lesson 2

Spaces at Home

Some artists paint **indoor spaces.**

Other artists paint **outdoor spaces.**

What kind of space is this?

Horace Pippin. *Victorian Parlor II*, 1945. Oil on canvas, 25¼ by 30 inches. The Metropolitan Museum of Art, Arthur Hoppock Hearn Fund, 1958 (58.26). Photograph © 1992 The Metropolitan Museum of Art, New York.

130

① Teach

Ask children to visualize their favorite room in their home. Ask volunteers to identify and describe the colors, textures, and lines in the room and tell what features make it their favorite.

Display page 130 and read the page aloud. Children should identify the space as an indoor space. Have children express any other ideas about the painting, such as, **It is a quiet and neat indoor space.** Ask:

- **How did the painter show balance?** (He made both sides about the same.)
- **What type of room is this?** (a sitting room) **What would a family do in this room?** (Possible responses: talk to each other; read books)

 Art Background

About the Artist Many of the paintings by American folk painter Horace Pippin (1888–1946) are visual memories of his childhood and his wartime experiences in World War I. A self-taught artist, he uses bold colors in his landscapes and shows biblical subjects and interiors.

 Notes

Lead children in a TPR (total physical response) activity in which they act out indoor and outdoor activities. Say: **Let's go outside. Open the door. Let's run! Throw the ball to me!**

Continue the activity by encouraging volunteers to suggest other indoor and outdoor activities that they would like to act out. Have them use words to accompany their activities.

130

Draw an Indoor Space

Studio 2

1. **Think.**

2. **Draw.**

3. **Add.**

4. **Color.**

Think Like an Artist

How did you make your space look special?

131

② Create

Explain to children that they will draw an indoor space. Invite them to look at the pictures as you point to and read the steps in the Studio. Encourage them to brainstorm real and imaginary places and to use a variety of colors and lines.

Technique Tip Using pencils and crayons, help children develop the skill of repeating lines or shapes to look like textures that might be found in a real indoor space.

 Quick Studio Have children draw an object or piece of furniture in their Sketchbook Journal that would be found in their favorite indoor space.

③ Close

Have children use the *Think Like an Artist* question to reflect on and express ideas about their own work. (Possible response: I used small lines to add soft textures.)

Ongoing Assessment

If . . . children need help to make their space unique,

then . . . encourage them to include a favorite toy or book in the space.

See page 108 from **Unit-by-Unit Resources** for a rubric to assess this studio.

 Fine Arts Connection

Dance Have children dance to show how they would feel and move in different spaces. For example, have them imagine they are inside a tiny room. Ask them to show what movements they would make inside such a small space. Then have them imagine they are outside in a huge field.

Meeting Individual Needs

Inclusion Children with low vision can add textured items to their indoor space, such as pieces of fabric, carpet scraps, or buttons. Invite them to tell about the space they drew and what the textured items represent.

Lesson 3

At a Glance

Objectives

- Identify and describe furniture.
- Bend pipe cleaners to make a piece of furniture.
- Respond to and make judgments about artworks.

Materials

- pipe cleaners , construction paper scraps, shoe boxes or other display materials
- Rubric 6 from **Unit-by-Unit Resources**

Vocabulary

furniture

NVAS (K–4) #1 Understanding and applying media, techniques, and processes

NVAS (K–4) #2 Using knowledge of structures and functions

NVAS (K–4) #6 Making connections between visual arts and other disciplines

---

Lesson 3

Furniture

A rocking chair is a type of **furniture.** Artists make furniture for people to use.

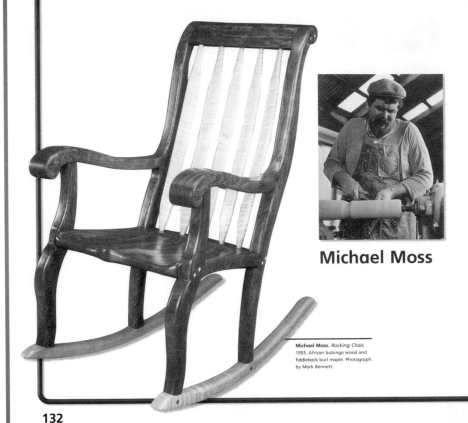

Michael Moss

Michael Moss. *Rocking Chair,* 1993. African bubinga wood and fiddleback burl maple. Photograph by Mark Bennett.

132

Teach

Play an Eye Spy game about furniture in the classroom. Point out the colors, textures, and forms of the furniture. For example, say: **I spy a piece of red furniture that you can sit on.** Have children identify the furniture and then take turns saying riddles.

Display page 132 and read the text aloud. Explain that the artist in the photograph made the rocking chair shown on the page. Tell children that artists like to create furniture because it is functional. Ask:

- **Do you like this rocking chair? Why?** (Possible response: Yes; I like the curved lines in the hand rails and the back of the chair.)

Art Background

Art History Furniture-making is a special form of art because the end result is a highly useful piece of sculpture. Drawing inspiration from nature, pop culture, and everyday life, today's furniture makers place equal emphasis on design, function, and workmanship.

ESL Notes

Display dollhouse furniture and furniture catalogs. Let children take turns choosing one piece of furniture to identify and then match to an item in the classroom or in a catalog. Some children may be able to tell how their furniture is used: **People put books on shelves.**

Make Wire Furniture

① Choose.

② Bend.

③ Twist.

④ Share.

Think Like an Artist

What was hard about making your furniture? What was easy?

133

Curriculum Connection

Math Have children take an inventory of furniture in the classroom. They can count the chairs, tables, and shelves. Help them decide how to list the information, in a graph, a chart, or an illustrated list.

 Meeting Individual Needs

Reteach Have children sketch a table or a chair before they make a piece of wire furniture. As they work, encourage them to describe the features of each—such as four legs, a horizontal surface, and so on.

② Create

Explain to children that they will arrange forms to make a piece of furniture from pipe cleaners and then place it in a miniature room.

Invite children to look at the pictures as you point to and read the steps in the Studio. Children who finish early might enjoy decorating a cut shoe box to look like the interior of a room.

Technique Tip Show children how to twist two pipe cleaner ends together to attach them.

Quick Studio Have children use modeling clay to make their furniture.

③ Close

Have children use the *Think Like an Artist* questions to express ideas about their own work. (Possible response: It was hard to make my chair stand up. The easy part was bending the corners.)

Provide an opportunity for children to express ideas about a portfolio, or a book, that shows several examples of artworks by an artist who creates furniture, such as Michael Moss. Model by saying: **Moss' portfolio includes many pieces of furniture made from the same materials.**

Ongoing Assessment

If . . . children have trouble manipulating the wire to look like a chair or a table,

then . . . suggest that they make the small parts of their furniture piece one at a time, and then put them together.

See page 108 from **Unit-by-Unit Resources** for a rubric to assess this studio.

Look and Compare

Look and Compare

At a Glance

Objectives

- Compare and contrast two artworks that tell a story.
- Respond to and make judgments about artworks.

Materials

- Art Prints 21, 22, 23

NVAS (K–4) #4 Understanding the visual arts in relation to history and cultures

NVAS (K–4) #5 Reflecting upon and assessing the characteristics and merits of their work and the work of others

Explore

Display **Art Print 21,** *Starry Crown.* Help children recall this painting by John Biggers from page 126. As children look at the two artworks on pages 134–135, invite them to predict which one was also created by Biggers, and give reasons for their answer. (*Jubilee*; Possible response: Some of the same symbols and patterns are used in both.)

Discuss

As you read the pages aloud, have children identify the subject of the two artworks. (One shows a group of people at a festival; one shows people building a palace.)

Explain that the people in the painting by Biggers are celebrating a harvest, a time when they gather food they have grown. The drawing on page 135 shows workers who lived hundreds of years ago, doing the kind of work they probably did almost every day.

Have children compare the two artworks describing which one they like the most and why. Remind children to be respectful of other classmates who may have differing opinions.

134

Art That Tells a Story

Many artworks show people together.

What might these people be celebrating?

Tell a story about the celebration.

John Biggers. *Jubilee.* Lake Wales Art Center, Lake Wales, FL.

134

 Art Background

Jubilee John Biggers was inspired to paint *Jubilee: Ghana Harvest Festival* after he returned from Africa in 1957. This huge mural is one of many works by Biggers that incorporates scenes from African life and symbols from African art and folklore.

About the Artist Persian manuscript painter Kamal al-Din Bihzad (1450–1535 or 1536) was important not only for the paintings he did during his lifetime, but also for the influence his work had on the evolution of painting in Persia, Asia, and India. His style is characterized by meticulously detailed pattern.

The workers in this drawing are building a palace.
Tell how these artworks are alike and different.

Attributed to Bihzad. *Building of the Palace of Khawarnaq,* ca. 1494. Manuscript drawing. By permission of The British Library, London (Or.6810.f.154.v).

135

 Reading Strategy

Draw Conclusions Tell children that when they read a story or look at an artwork, they sometimes draw conclusions. This means that they use clues from the story or picture, as well as what they already know, to figure out something that is not said or shown.

Create an exhibition of Biggers' artworks by using **Art Print 21,** *Starry Crown,* and **Art Print 22,** *Jubilee.* Find other artworks by John Biggers and display them in the classroom. Encourage children to draw conclusions about Biggers' artworks after looking at the exhibition. Model by saying: **Biggers paints many artworks about people. He uses different African symbols in his paintings.** Invite children to draw their own conclusions about the exhibit. Have them express any other ideas about the artworks.

Apply

Draw a Venn diagram like the one below on the chalkboard. Tell children that this graphic organizer is a good way to show how two artworks are the same and different.

To fill in the diagram, suggest that children first compare the artworks, looking for ways they are alike. Fill in the middle section as children suggest ideas.

Guide children as they look for differences by suggesting that they focus on the actions of the two artworks. Possible responses are shown in blue.

Art That Tells a Story

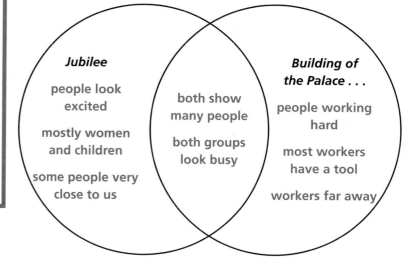

Jubilee

people look excited

mostly women and children

some people very close to us

both show many people

both groups look busy

Building of the Palace . . .

people working hard

most workers have a tool

workers far away

Close

Ask children what they learned about artworks that tell a story. (Possible response: An artist can choose how many people he or she wants to show, and also decide what each one is doing.)

Lesson 4

At a Glance

Objectives

- Identify and describe characteristics of a mural.
- Use crayons to create a mural.
- Respond to and make judgments about artworks.

Materials

- tape, butcher paper, crayons or markers
- Rubric 6 from **Unit-by-Unit Resources**

Vocabulary

murals

NVAS (K–4) #1 Understanding and applying media, techniques, and processes

NVAS (K–4) #2 Using knowledge of structures and functions

NVAS (K–4) #3 Choosing and evaluating a range of subject matter, symbols, and ideas

NVAS (K–4) #6 Making connections between visual arts and other disciplines

① Teach

Have children discuss their favorite subjects. Prompt them by asking questions such as: **What is your favorite sport or activity? What part of the school day is your favorite?** Say, for example, **I enjoy gardening.**

Display and read page 136 aloud. Explain that artists choose subjects from the environment that they want to express ideas and feelings about in artworks. To help children understand the subject of the mural, point to and read the credit line. Explain that miners are workers who get coal, rocks, and metal from under the ground. Ask:

- **What is most interesting to you about this artwork?** (Possible response: I like how the artist showed a different movement with each miner.)

Murals

Some artists paint artworks on walls.

These artworks are called **murals.**

What is the subject of this mural?

Diego Rivera. *Surface Miners,* 1923. Mural, 166 by 82 inches. Court of Labor, Level 1, South Wall, Secretaria de Educacion Publica, Mexico City, Mexico.

136

 Art Background

About the Artist Mexican artist Diego Rivera (1886–1957) is best known for his murals depicting the political and social movements of Mexico's history. He was a master of the fresco technique, in which paint is applied directly onto fresh plaster.

 Notes

Lead children to act out different workers using their tools. As you act out, for example, a miner with a pickax or a shovel, say: **I am a miner. I split rocks. I pick them up with my shovel.** Encourage children to repeat your sentences as they join in the actions.

Make a Mural

1 Plan.

2 Draw. Make it big!

3 Color.

4 Share.

Think Like an Artist

How did you and your friends make the mural?

137

 Curriculum Connection

Health Remind children that muralists paint subjects that are important to them. Tell children that they are going to make a door mural with a health topic that is important to them, such as eating healthy foods to help them grow or taking care of their teeth.

Cover a door with butcher paper, and invite children to draw pictures that show their subject matter.

 Meeting Individual Needs

Inclusion Encourage children with low vision to help in the planning and coloring of the oversize figures in the mural.

---

2 Create

Explain that small groups of children will make a mural of people working. To brainstorm ideas, suggest that they think of work they do at home.

Point to and read the steps in the Studio. Explain that in Step 1, group members need to agree on their subject and then map out how they will show it in a mural. Remind children to create their mural using a variety of colors and lines.

Technique Tip Let children use pencils to sketch where objects and people will be placed on the butcher paper.

Quick Studio Have each child draw their own mural on large construction paper or newsprint.

3 Close

Have children use the *Think Like an Artist* question to reflect on their own work. (Possible response: We decided what kind of work to show. Then we planned our picture, drew it, and colored it in.)

Ongoing Assessment

If . . . children have trouble agreeing on a subject,

then . . . listen to their ideas and help them decide which one would be easiest to draw.

See page 108 from **Unit-by-Unit Resources** for a rubric to assess this studio.

Lesson 5

At a Glance

Objectives

- Identify and describe the subject of an artwork.
- Use pencils and crayons to show a game.
- Respond to and make judgments about artworks.

Materials

- photographs of people playing indoor and outdoor games (optional)
- drawing paper, pencils, crayons
- Rubric 6 from **Unit-by-Unit Resources**

NVAS (K–4) #1 Understanding and applying media, techniques, and processes

NVAS (K–4) #2 Using knowledge of structures and functions

NVAS (K–4) #3 Choosing and evaluating a range of subject matter, symbols, and ideas

NVAS (K–4) #6 Making connections between visual arts and other disciplines

Teach

Ask children what games they like to play, both indoors and outdoors. Discuss what makes each game fun, and what skills you need to play it. Have children describe the games by naming forms or colors associated with it. For example, say: **I like soccer. The ball is a round form.**

Explain to children that some artists like to make playing games their subject. Then display and read page 138. Point out that the game is unusual because animals, not people, are the players. Children may say the lion is winning because it is smiling. Ask:

- **What subject would you like to create an artwork about?** (hide and go seek) **Why?** (That is my favorite outdoor game.)

Lesson 5

Games

What is unusual about the game in this painting?

Who might be winning?

How do you know?

Artist unknown. *A Lion and Antelope Play Senet,* 1250–1150 B.C. Mineral pigments on Egyptian papyrus, height 3½ inches. Reproduced courtesy of The Trustees of The British Museum, London.

Art Background

Art History In this scene from the *Satirical Papyrus,* a lion and an antelope play the ancient Egyptian board game of Senet, the predecessor of backgammon. The lion has a greedy, self-satisfied look, as if he expects to win the game. This papyrus is unusual because of its amusing, satirical overtones.

ESL Notes

Display board games, such as checkers or chess. If any children have played these games, encourage them to demonstrate some moves. Then invite children to tell about other indoor games they play.

Studio 5

Draw a Game

1. **Think.**

2. **Draw.**

3. **Add.**

4. **Color.**

Think Like an Artist

What do you like best about your picture?

139

 Curriculum Connection

Social Studies Have children make a class memory game. Have each child draw the same object on two separate index cards. Place all of the cards face down on the table. Invite volunteers to turn over two cards looking for a match. If a match is found, the player picks up the two cards, and continues. The player with the most cards at the end of the game, wins. After playing the game, ask: **What happens if a player peeks at a card before turning it over?**

 Meeting Individual Needs

Extend Have children choose another game that two (or more) animals might play. Ask children to draw their game ideas in their Sketchbook Journals.

② Create

Display pictures of indoor and outdoor games, and tell children they will draw themselves playing a game. Ask several volunteers to tell what game they will draw.

Invite children to look at the steps in the Studio as you explain them. Explain that in Step 3, children should add lines, colors, and shapes to make their picture more interesting.

Technique Tip Tell children that by pressing hard with their crayon, they can make brighter, bolder colors. Pressing gently makes softer colors.

Quick Studio Have children use chalk on a chalkboard or outside to draw themselves playing a game.

③ Close

Have children use the *Think Like an Artist* question to express ideas about their own work. (Possible response: I like how I am playing with my dog.)

Ongoing Assessment

If . . . children have trouble visualizing their game,

then . . . have them talk to a friend who knows how to play the same game.

See page 108 from **Unit-by-Unit Resources** for a rubric to assess this studio.

Lesson 6

At a Glance

Objectives

- Identify and describe contrast in colors.
- Use crayons and paint to make a crayon resist.
- Respond to and make judgments about artworks.

Materials

- dark-color crayons, drawing paper, wide paintbrushes, diluted light-color tempera paint
- Rubric 6 from **Unit-by-Unit Resources**

Vocabulary

contrast

NVAS (K–4) #1 Understanding and applying media, techniques, and processes

NVAS (K–4) #2 Using knowledge of structures and functions

NVAS (K–4) #3 Choosing and evaluating a range of subject matter, symbols, and ideas

NVAS (K–4) #6 Making connections between visual arts and other disciplines

Lesson 6

People at Play

What do you see first in this painting?
This artist used **contrast** in the colors.
He put light colors next to dark colors.

Paul Gauguin. *Breton Girls Dancing, Pont-Aven*, 1888. Oil on canvas, 28¾ by 36½ inches. National Gallery of Art, Washington, D.C., collection of Mr. and Mrs. Paul Mellon. Photograph © 1997 Board of Trustees, National Gallery of Art, Washington, D.C.

140

① Teach

Point out examples of light and dark colors together, such as in a child's clothing or in artwork on the wall. Have children identify other examples of light and dark colors.

Display and read page 140 aloud. Children may say they notice the girls' heads and faces first. Help them understand that artists put light colors next to dark colors to make the light colors stand out. Say:

- **Point to the dark colors in the painting.** (the girls' dresses and aprons, the dog, the trees in the background)
- **Do you like how the artist used colors in this painting? Why?** (Possible response: Yes, I like it because it makes the girl's clothes stand out.)

 Art Background

About the Artist Post-impressionist painter Paul Gauguin (1848–1903) was drawn to the simple country life of Brittany, France, returning there to paint in 1886, 1888, and 1889. In the village of Pont Aven, he painted the rural lifestyle of the Breton people, drawing inspiration from their distinctive customs and costumes.

ESL Notes

Choose a light and dark crayon for primary and secondary colors. Place them in a row in front of children and name them together—light blue, dark green, and so on. Ask children to hide their eyes while you remove one color. Encourage everyone to call out the missing color.

140

Make a Crayon Resist

Studio 6

1 Choose.

2 Press hard.

3 Add.

4 Paint.

Think Like an Artist

Which part of your artwork stands out? Why?

141

2 Create

In advance, display a simple crayon resist and have children describe how they think it was made. Tell them they will make their own crayon resist.

Have children follow along as you read the steps in the Studio. In Step 2, tell children that they can draw a subject from real life or an idea from their imagination.

Technique Tip Tell children that the harder they press with their crayons, the brighter their crayon resist will be, because of the contrast with the light paint.

Quick Studio Have children write their name with a white crayon on yellow or white paper, and then paint over it with dark paint.

3 Close

Have children use the *Think Like an Artist* questions to express ideas about their own work. (Possible response: the parts where I pressed down hard with a black crayon)

Ongoing Assessment

If . . . children have trouble seeing the crayon lines after they paint,

then . . . add more water to the paint or tell them to press harder in a new picture.

See page 108 from **Unit-by-Unit Resources** for a rubric to assess this studio.

 Fine Arts Connection

Music Point out to children that musicians and composers also use contrast to add interest. Play or sing a song with a surprise ending, such as "Pop! Goes the Weasel." Point out that up to the word *Pop!*, all the words are sung at about the same tempo and loudness. The song is fun to sing because of the contrast that the word *Pop* provides.

 Meeting Individual Needs

Inclusion For children who have trouble focusing their attention, separate the two parts of the Studio so that children draw with crayons at one table and then go to another table to paint over their picture.

Artist at Work

At a Glance

Objectives
- Read about a career in art.
- Identify the use of art in everyday life.
- Relate art to personal experiences.

Materials
- origami (optional)
- Sketchbook Journals

Vocabulary
origami

NVAS (K–4) #5 Reflecting upon and assessing the characteristics and merits of their work and the work of others

Explore

Display an example of origami and invite children to describe how they think it was made. (Possible response: from cut and folded paper) Explain that the special paper origami artists use is very similar to the paper they use in their everyday lives. Origami paper is thinner and comes in a variety of colors. Children could still use paper from their classroom if they would like to make some simple shapes.

Discuss

Read aloud pages 142 and 143. Ask:

- **What materials does Fukumoto use to make origami artworks?** (special paper and scissors)
- **Where do you think Fukumoto gets her ideas?** (Possible response: She might choose animals, plants, and objects from her environment.)
- **What type of job could an origami artist do?** (Possible response: An origami artist could teach other people how to do origami or create decorations or gifts.)

Folded Paper

Jodi Fukumoto makes **origami.**

She cut and folded special paper to make these artworks.

Which origami is your favorite? Why?

Jodi Fukumoto

142

 Career Research

Tell children that many people enjoy working with their hands to make things for their home or for other people to buy and enjoy. Ask them to think about crafts or hobbies that they have seen family members or neighbors do, such as woodworking, quilting, and so on. Make a chart that shows crafts and hobbies children mention, and encourage children to bring examples of some from home.

origami birds

Origami looks easy to make, but each
fold and cut must be exactly right.
It might take hours to make just one.

143

 Reading Strategy

Identify Cause and Effect Relationships Remind
children that when they read a story or look at an
artwork, it helps to think about causes and effects. Display
a square of paper and tell children that you will use it to
make a hat.

As you begin folding corners and sides, pause after each
step and ask children why you made the fold, and what
will happen as a result. When the hat is done, review with
children how each fold you made created an important
part of the hat.

Apply

Tell children that they are going to write a letter to
Jodi Fukomoto asking her about her origami.
Create a class chart with children to list questions
they would like to include in their letter. Possible
responses are shown below.

Questions
1. Where can we find special paper to make origami?
2. What was the largest size origami artwork you have made? What was the smallest?
3. What do you do with your artworks once you finish?

After children have completed their list, write a
class letter incorporating their questions.

Close

Review the completed list and ask: **What object
would you like to create in origami? Why?**
(Possible response: I would like to create a frog.
I would give it to my little brother because he
loves frogs.)

Sketchbook Journal Invite children to draw an
object or an animal that they would like to see in
an origami.

Portfolio Project

At a Glance

Objectives

- Develop and organize ideas from the environment.
- Evaluate original artworks by self and others.

Materials

- chain-link fence or indoor loom
- fabric scraps cut in long strips
- ribbons, crêpe paper, yarn, twine
- long grass stems
- Rubric 6 from **Unit-by-Unit Resources**

NVAS (K–4) #1 Understanding and applying media, techniques, and processes

NVAS (K–4) #3 Choosing and evaluating a range of subject matter, symbols, and ideas

NVAS (K–4) #5 Reflecting upon and assessing the characteristics and merits of their work and the work of others

Portfolio Project

Weave a Fence

1 Plan.

2 Gather.

3 Weave.

4 Tell a story.

144

Plan

Find a chain-link fence to serve as a loom in this outdoor art project. If working indoors, create a loom on a bulletin board by tacking lengths of yarn so that they hang vertically at children's eye level.

Explain to children that they will make an artwork by weaving long pieces of fabric or grass through the holes in a fence. Show children some of the materials they can weave. Ask:

- **What is your subject or theme?**
- **What materials will you use?**
- **What colors will you use?**

Quick Project

Have children weave ribbons and other materials through vertical strips of construction paper to create a placemat.

👪 Meeting Individual Needs

Extend Encourage children to make some of the materials they will weave. For example, they might tie simple knots in a long piece of twine before they weave it through the fence.

Inclusion Children who are visually impaired will enjoy this tactile project and should be able to participate fully.

Look at these outdoor murals.

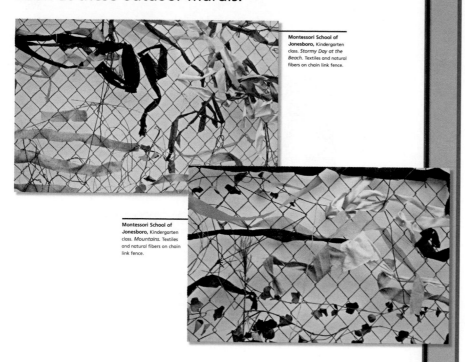

Montessori School of Jonesboro, Kindergarten class. *Stormy Day at the Beach.* Textiles and natural fibers on chain link fence.

Montessori School of Jonesboro, Kindergarten class. *Mountains.* Textiles and natural fibers on chain link fence.

Share Your Art

1. What does your mural show?
2. How do the different materials make your mural special?

145

 Gallery Options

Weaving Exhibition Help the small groups create name cards that list the title, the group members, and the materials used. Attach the cards to the weavings.

Invite another class to see the exhibition of weavings. Pair each child with a guest. Ask them to express ideas about the weavings in the exhibition. Model by saying: **The weavings in this exhibit were all made with a variety of materials. Each weaving has its own unique theme.**

Create

Gather the materials and guide children through the steps on page 144 to complete the project.

- Encourage children to think of a theme, such as the American flag or the seashore.
- If possible, take children on a walk to collect some natural weaving materials. Otherwise, have weaving materials already collected for children.
- Tell children to arrange their strips before they begin to weave. Since weaving materials will be different lengths, tell children to expect uneven edges. Some children may want to fill in gaps with additional grasses, ribbons, or crêpe paper.
- Let children take turns telling a story about their weaving, or explaining how they made it.

Close

Ask children to express ideas about the artworks shown on page 145. Model by saying, **This kindergarten class used a beach theme. I like how they used the colors found at the beach.**

Have children express ideas about a peer's artwork by answering the following questions.

- **What is interesting about these weavings?** (Possible response: the many different fabrics and fibers that the children used)
- **How are these weavings like yours?** (Answers will vary.)

Use the *Share Your Art* questions to help children express ideas about their own artwork. (Answers will vary.)

See page 108 from **Unit-by-Unit Resources** for a rubric to assess this project.

Unit 6 Review

At a Glance

Objectives

- Relate art terms to the environment.
- Identify murals, furniture, origami, and architect.
- Describe, analyze, interpret, and judge an artwork.

Materials

- **Art Print 24**
- children's art portfolios

NVAS (K–4) #1 Understanding and applying media, techniques, and processes

NVAS (K–4) #2 Using knowledge of structures and functions

NVAS (K–4) #5 Reflecting upon and assessing the characteristics and merits of their work and the work of others

Think About Art

Responses:

mural (Point to the mural.)
furniture (Point to the furniture.)
origami (Point to the origami.)
architect (Point to the architect.)

Talk About Art

Organize children into groups of three or four. Have children choose a favorite artwork from their portfolio to share with the group. Prompt children to tell a story about their artworks.

After each child shares their artwork, invite group members to express their ideas about it. Remind children to show respect for everyone's opinion. When a child offers a differing opinion, model a respectful response by saying: **Thank you for sharing. I'll think about that as I create other artworks.**

Think About Art

Match each word with a picture.

mural   **furniture**   **origami**   **architect**

Talk About Art

- Choose an artwork that you enjoyed making.
- Tell a friend how you made it.

146

 Assessment Options

Options for assessing children appear in the **Unit-by-Unit Resources.**

- Use the **Vocabulary Worksheets** on pages 101–104 for an informal assessment of Unit 6 vocabulary.
- Use the **Unit 6 Test** on pages 109–112 to assess children's mastery of unit vocabulary and concepts.

Natalia Goncharova. *The Harvest*, ca. 1909. Oil on canvas. Russian State Museum, St. Petersburg, Russia. Scala/Art Resource, New York. © 1998 Artists Rights Society (ARS), New York/ADAGP, Paris.

Put It All Together

1. What do you see?

2. Why did the artist use light and dark colors?

3. How do you think the workers feel about their jobs?

4. Which part is most interesting? Why?

147

Put It All Together

Use the questions on page 147 to evaluate the artwork. Possible responses follow.

1. a painting of people working in a field DESCRIBE
2. to make the people stand out ANALYZE
3. They probably think their jobs are very hard work. INTERPRET
4. the workers' scarves, because they are all different JUDGE

 Art Background

About the Artist Russian artist Natalia Goncharova (1881–1962) was a painter, graphic artist, book illustrator, and theatre designer. She was part of the Russian Avant-Garde movement which flourished from the turn of the century to the mid-1930's. Goncharova was influenced by Russian icons, Russian primitive and folk art, and Futurism. Throughout her career she worked as a set and costume designer for several theatre and ballet companies.

Picture Glossary

A

architect
page 128

art
page 18

Franz Marc. *The Large Blue Horses*, 1911.

artist
page 20

B

balance
page 92

beads
page 108

C

camera
page 84

148

color wheel
page 48

colors
page 28

contrast
page 140

cool colors
page 30

E

express
page 116

F

form
page 62

furniture
page 132

149

I

illustrations

page 32

imagination

page 72

indoor space

page 130

Carmen Lomas Garza. *Empanadas*, 1991.

L

letters

page 110

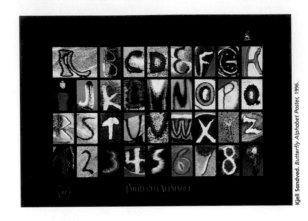

Kjell Sandved. *Butterfly Alphabet Poster*, 1996.

lines

page 20

M

mask

page 118

mobile
page 76

Gabe Stoner and Mike Hatton, *Vito Calzone*, 1999.

movement
page 96

mural
page 136

N

nature
page 94

O

origami
page 142

outdoor space
page 130

P

paintbrush
page 42

pattern
page 50

photograph

page 84

print

page 86

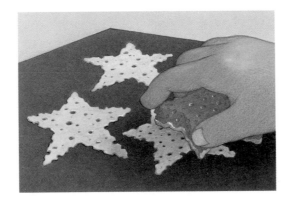

puppet

page 70

recycle

page 74

sculpture

page 64

Artist unknown, Yoruba People. *Beaded Crown*, late 19th century

senses

page 26

shapes

page 22

space
page 66

subject
page 52

symbol
page 106

 T

texture
page 40

 W

warm colors
page 30

weaver
page 88

153

Acknowledgments

ILLUSTRATIONS

19, 21, 23, 27, 29, 31, 41, 43, 45, 49, 51, 53, 58, 63, 65, 67, 71, 73, 75, 80, 85, 87, 89, 93, 95, 97, 102, 107, 109, 111, 115, 117, 119, 124, 129, 131, 133, 137, 139, 141, 151, 153 Meredith Johnson

34, 56, 78, 100, 122, 144 Linda Hill Griffith

148, 150, 152 Anni Matsick

PHOTOGRAPHS

Every effort has been made to secure permission and provide appropriate credit for photographic material. The publisher deeply regrets any omission and pledges to correct errors called to its attention in subsequent editions.

Unless otherwise acknowledged, all photographs are the property of Scott Foresman, a division of Pearson Education.

Photo locators denoted as follows: Top (t), Center (c), Bottom (b), Left (l), Right (r), Background (Bkgd)

Front Matter
Page iv, © The Solomon R. Guggenheim Foundation, New York; 7, © SuperStock; 10, © 1996 Board of Trustees, National Gallery of Art, Washington, D.C. Gift of Mrs. John W. Simpson.

Units 1–6
Page 17(bl), Albrecht Dürer. *Self-Portrait at Age 28,* 1500. Oil on wood, 26 1/8 by 19 1/8 inches. Alte Pinakothek, Munich, Germany. Giraudon/Art Resource, NY; 18, © P.J. Wagner/Getty Images; 22, © 2004 Succession H. Matisse, Paris/Artists Rights Society (ARS), New York; 24, © Erich Lessing/Art Resource, NY; 28, Solomon R. Guggenheim Museum, New York, Gift of Solomon R. Guggenheim, 1937, 37.446. © 2004 Artists Rights Society (ARS), New York/ADAGP, Paris; 32(b), From *Under My Nose* by Lois Ehlert. Photographs by Carlo Ontal. Appears courtesy/Richard C. Owen Publishers, Inc., Katonah, NY 10536; 33(cr), 33(bl), Harper-Collins Childrens Publishers; 36(cr), © Getty Images; 37, © Stefano Bianchetti/Corbis. © 2004 Artists Rights Society (ARS), New York/ADAGP, Paris; 38, National Gallery of Art/Bridgeman Art Library. © 2004 Estate of Pablo Picasso/Artists Rights Society (ARS), New York; 39(bl), Pablo Picasso. *Yo, Picasso (Self-Portrait),* 1901. Oil on canvas, 29 by 23⅜ inches. Private collection. Art Resource, NY. © 2004 Estate of Pablo Picasso/Artist Rights Society (ARS), New York; 39(bc), © Getty Images; 39(br), © Weinberg/Clark/Getty Images; 40, © Pat O'Hara/Corbis; 44, © Smithsonian American Art Museum, Washington, D.C./Art Resource, NY. © Helen Frankenthaler; 46, © Réunion des Musées Nationaux/Art Resource, NY; 48, Gift of the T.B. Walker Foundation, Gilbert M. Walker Fund, 1942/Collection Walker Art Center, Minneapolis; 54(c), 54(bl), 55(br), Carolyn Bennett; 61(bl), © Christopher Felver/Corbis; 61(b), © Getty Images; 62, © Dave Bartruff/Corbis; 68, © 2004 Marisol Escobar/Licensed by VAGA, New York, NY; 70, Photograph by Blair Clark; 72, © Deborah Butterfield; 74, National Museum of American Art, Smithsonian Institution, Washington, D.C./Art Resource, NY; 76, © Jerry Anthony/Gabe Stoner and Michael Hatton; 76, © Tim Flach/Getty Images; 77, © Gabe Stoner and Michael Hatton; 77, © SuperStock; 77, © ThinkStock/SuperStock; 80, © Paul Meyer/Index Stock Imagery; 80(bl), Goose Rocks Designs © 2003; 82, Digital image © The Museum of Modern Art/Licensed by Scala/Art Resource, NY; 83(bl), Vincent van Gogh. *Self-Portrait,* 1887. MEDIUM, SIZE. Musée d'Orsay, Paris, France. Scala/Art Resource, NY; 83(bc), © C Squared Studios/Getty Images; 84, © Ariel Skelley/Corbis; 88, © Jack Fields/Corbis; 90, © Erich Lessing/Art Resource, NY; 92(r), © John Bigelow Taylor/Art Resource, NY; 94, © Digital Stock; 94, © Digital Stock; 94, © Corbis; 98, © Jose Sainz; 102, © Cooperphoto, Inc./Corbis; 102, © Lindsay Hebberd/Corbis; 105(b), © Duncan Smith/Getty Images; 105(bc), © Seide Preis/Getty Images; 105(br), © Arthur S. Aubry/Getty Images; 105(br), © David Toase/Getty Images; 105(bl), Photo © Ann Oppenhimer; 106, © Charles E. Rotkin/Corbis; 110, © Terry Eggers/Corbis; 110(t), © Kjell B. Sandved. For more information call 1-800-ABC-WING; 112, Collection of John and Diane Balsley/Photo: Courtesy Patrick and Beatrice Haggerty Museum of Art/Marquette University, Milwaukee, WI; 113, Girard Foundation Collection. Museum of International Folk Art, Santa Fe, NM. Photo by Michel Monteaux; 114, © Jane Wooster Scott/SuperStock; 116(t), © Mark Fortenberry Photography; 120, 121, Akari Light Sculpture, Michio Noguchi. Reproduced with the permission of the Isamu Noguchi Foundation, Inc. NY; 124(tc), © Jan Cook/Getty Images; 124(br), © Felicia Martinez/PhotoEdit; 124(cr), © Getty Images; 124(tr), © Corbis; 127, © Bob Krist/Corbis; 127, © Lindsay Hebberd/Corbis; 127(bl), Photo by Earlie Hudnall, Hudnall's Positive Images; 128, © Catherine Karnow/Corbis; 132(l), Photograph by Marc Bennett; 134, Photo by Earlie Hudnall, Hudnall's Positive Images; 136, © Schalkwijk/Art Resource, NY. © Fiduciario en el Fideicomiso relativo a los Museos Diego Rivera y Frida Kahlo. Reproduction authorized by the Bank of Mexico, Mexico City; 142, 143, Product Development Dept. The Guide to Hawaiian-Style Origami Charms Copyright 2003, Island Heritage Publishing; 143, © Fukuhara, Inc./Corbis; 146, © Getty Images; 146, © George Disario/Corbis; 146, © Philip Harvey/Corbis.

Back Matter
148 (tl) © David Young-Wolff/Photo Edit; 148 (cl) © Gift of the T.B. Walker Foundation, Gilbert M. Walker Fund, 1942/Collection Walker Art Center, Minneapolis; 148 (bl) © Lifestyles Today; 148 (bc) © Getty Images; 148 (tr) © Dave Bartruff/Corbis; 149 (bl) © Schafer/Smith/SuperStock; 149 (br) © Canadian Museum of Civilization/Corbis; 150 (bl) © 1991 Carmen Lomas Garza. Collection of Romeo Montaluo, M. D., Brownsville, TX. Photograph by Judy Reed.; 150 (br) © Arthur Tilley/Getty Images; 151 (bl) © David Robinson/Corbis; 151 (tr) © Santokh Kochar/Getty Images; 151 (cr) © Fukahara, Inc./Corbis; 151 (cr) © Peter Barrett/Corbis; 152 (tl) © Wolfgang Kaehler/Corbis; 152 (bl) © SW Productions/Getty Images; 152 (tr) © Robert Ginn/Photo Edit; 153 (tl) © Corbis; 153 (bl) © Corbis; 153 (cr) © Corbis; 153 (br) © Keren Su/Corbis.

154

Scope and Sequence

Artistic Perception
Awareness and sensitivity to natural and human-made environments

Concepts
Students progressively learn that their multisensory experiences, such as hearing, touching, moving, and seeing, can help them perceive and identify the visual elements of art as well as the visual principles of design.

Legend

○ Open circles indicate the grade where aspects are introduced.

● Shaded circles indicate the grades where aspects are developed.

		Levels								
		K	1	2	3	4	5	6	7	8
Elements of Art	**Line**									
Explore and examine line in art		○	●	●	●	●	●	●	●	●
Identify and name types of lines such as curved, straight, thick, thin, fine, broad, dotted, wavy, zigzag, continuous, broken		○	●	●	●	●	●	●	●	●
Use a variety of art media and tools to create line		○	●	●	●	●	●	●	●	●
Recognize horizontal, vertical, and diagonal lines					○	●	●	●	●	●
Recognize actual and implied lines						○	●	●	●	●
Use line to create shape or form		○	●	●	●	●	●	●	●	●
Use line to create pattern and texture		○	●	●	●	●	●	●	●	●
Use line to create movement		○	●	●	●	●	●	●	●	●
Use line to express thoughts and emotions		○	●	●	●	●	●	●	●	●
Name, identify, and use line as an element of art		○	●	●	●	●	●	●	●	●
	Color									
Explore and examine color in art		○	●	●	●	●	●	●	●	●
Name and identify warm colors and use them in a composition		○	●	●	●	●	●	●	●	●
Name and identify cool colors and use them in a composition		○	●	●	●	●	●	●	●	●
Name and identify primary and secondary colors		○	●	●	●	●	●	●	●	●
Mix primary colors to make secondary colors		○	●	●	●	●	●	●	●	●
Name and identify intermediate colors					○	●	●	●	●	●
Mix primary colors with secondary colors to make intermediate colors			○	●	●	●	●	●	●	●
Name, identify, and use neutrals such as white, black, gray					○	●	●	●	●	●
Name, identify, and use color schemes: harmonies				○	●	●	●	●	●	●
Recognize properties of color such as hue, value, intensity					○	●	●	●	●	●
Name, identify, and use color as an element of art		○	●	●	●	●	●	●	●	●

Scope and Sequence

	Levels								
	K	1	2	3	4	5	6	7	8
Value									
Explore and examine value in art		○	●	●	●	●	●	●	●
Recognize value as being the lightness or darkness of a color		○	●	●	●	●	●	●	●
Create color tints	○	●	●	●	●	●	●	●	●
Create color shades	○	●	●	●	●	●	●	●	●
Name, identify, and use value as an element of art		○	●	●	●	●	●	●	●
Shape									
Explore and examine shape in art	○	●	●	●	●	●	●	●	●
Recognize shape as being a two-dimensional flat space enclosed by actual or implied lines	○	●	●	●	●	●	●	●	
Identify organic shapes		○	●	●	●	●	●	●	●
Name and identify geometric shapes	○	●	●	●	●	●	●	●	●
Arrange shapes to create a work of art	○	●	●	●	●	●	●	●	●
Use shape to create pattern and texture	○	●	●	●	●	●	●	●	●
Name, identify, and use shape as an element of art		○	●	●	●	●	●	●	●
Texture									
Explore and examine texture in art	○	●	●	●	●	●	●	●	●
Recognize texture as the look and/or feel of a surface	○	●	●	●	●	●	●	●	●
Name and identify different types of textures	○	●	●	●	●	●	●	●	●
Distinguish between tactile and visual texture			○	●	●	●	●	●	●
Create texture in a work of art	○	●	●	●	●	●	●	●	●
Name, identify, and use texture as an element of art		○	●	●	●	●	●	●	●
Form									
Explore and examine form in art	○	●	●	●	●	●	●	●	●
Recognize form as being a three-dimensional object with height, width, and depth	○	●	●	●	●	●	●	●	●
Identify organic forms		○	●	●	●	●	●	●	●
Name and identify geometric forms	○	●	●	●	●	●	●	●	●
Arrange forms to create a work of art	○	●	●	●	●	●	●	●	●
Name, identify, and use form as an element of art	○	●	●	●	●	●	●	●	●

	Levels								
	K	1	2	3	4	5	6	7	8
Space									
Explore and examine space in art	○	●	●	●	●	●	●	●	●
Recognize that space is the actual or visual area within and around shapes and forms: foreground, middle ground, background		○	●	●	●	●	●	●	●
Recognize positive space		○	●	●	●	●	●	●	●
Recognize negative space		○	●	●	●	●	●	●	●
Work with space in a work of art	○	●	●	●	●	●	●	●	●
Name, identify, and use space as an element of art	○	●	●	●	●	●	●	●	●
Principles of Design **Unity**									
Explore and examine unity in art			○	●	●	●	●	●	●
Recognize that unity in a work of art is a quality that occurs when all its elements and principles are working together			○	●	●	●	●	●	●
Name and identify the elements and/or principles in a work of art that create unity				○	●	●	●	●	●
Understand and use unity as a principle of design			○	●	●	●	●	●	●
Variety									
Explore and examine variety in art			○	●	●	●	●	●	●
Recognize that variety in a work of art is a change in shape, form, appearance, or detail that creates interest				○	●	●	●	●	●
Recognize that unity and variety often work together in design				○	●	●	●	●	●
Understand and use variety as a principle of design			○	●	●	●	●	●	●
Emphasis									
Explore and examine emphasis in art		○	●	●	●	●	●	●	●
Recognize that emphasis implies areas in a work of art that dominate and draw attention to the main idea		○	●	●	●	●	●	●	●
Identify emphasis in works of art		○	●	●	●	●	●	●	●
Understand and use emphasis as a principle of design		○	●	●	●	●	●	●	●

Legend

○ Open circles indicate the grade where aspects are introduced.

● Shaded circles indicate the grades where aspects are developed.

Scope and Sequence

	Levels								
	K	**1**	**2**	**3**	**4**	**5**	**6**	**7**	**8**
Balance									
Explore and examine balance in art	○	●	●	●	●	●	●	●	●
Recognize that balance is a way of arranging elements of design to give an artwork a sense of equality in visual weight	○	●	●	●	●	●	●	●	●
Identify symmetrical balance	○	●	●	●	●	●	●	●	●
Identify radial balance			○	●	●	●	●	●	●
Identify asymmetrical balance			○	●	●	●	●	●	●
Understand and use balance as a principle of design	○	●	●	●	●	●	●	●	●
Proportion									
Explore and examine proportion in art			○	●	●	●	●	●	●
Recognize that proportion is the size relationship of one part to the whole			○	●	●	●	●	●	●
Recognize that proportion can indicate distance			○	●	●	●	●	●	●
Understand and use proportion as a principle of design			○	●	●	●	●	●	●
Pattern									
Explore and examine pattern in art	○	●	●	●	●	●	●	●	●
Recognize that pattern is an arrangement of lines, shapes, colors, or forms in a regular repetition	○	●	●	●	●	●	●	●	●
Understand and use pattern as a principle of design	○	●	●	●	●	●	●	●	●
Rhythm									
Explore and examine rhythm in art			○	●	●	●	●	●	●
Recognize that rhythm is a sense of visual movement achieved by the repetition of one or more elements of art in a work of art				○	●	●	●	●	●
Recognize types of rhythm: random, regular, alternating, flowing, progressive							●	●	●
Understand and use rhythm as a principle of design				○	●	●	●	●	●

Creative Art Process

Inventive and imaginative expression through art materials and tools

○ Open circles indicate the grade where aspects are introduced.

● Shaded circles indicate the grades where aspects are developed.

Concepts

Students progressively learn to experiment with art materials in order to understand properties and develop manipulative skills and in order to express individual ideas, thoughts, and feelings in simple media.

			Levels							
		K	1	2	3	4	5	6	7	8
Media and Methods	**Drawing**									
Express individual ideas, thoughts, and feelings through drawing		○	●	●	●	●	●	●	●	●
Draw with a variety of materials such as pencils, crayons, pastels, chalk, water-based pens		○	●	●	●	●	●	●	●	●
Draw from memory, imagination, or observation		○	●	●	●	●	●	●	●	●
Create an artwork using a variety of drawing materials, such as charcoal, pen and ink								○	●	●
	Collage, Mosaic, and Mixed Media									
Express individual ideas, thoughts, and feelings through collage, mosaic, and mixed media		○	●	●	●	●	●	●	●	●
Create a collage using a variety of materials such as paper, found objects, cardboard, string, plastic, fiber		○	●	●	●	●	●	●	●	●
Create a mosaic using a variety of materials such as pieces of tile, construction-paper pieces, small stones			○	●	●	●	●	●	●	●
Create a mixed-media artwork using a variety of materials such as photographs, magazine pictures, paper, yarn, paint, crayons		○	●	●	●	●	●	●	●	●
	Painting									
Express individual ideas, thoughts, and feelings through painting		○	●	●	●	●	●	●	●	●
Create an artwork using a variety of painting tools and materials such as tempera or liquid school acrylic, brushes, string, fingers, sponges, found objects, paper		○	●	●	●	●	●	●	●	●
	Printmaking									
Express individual ideas, thoughts, and feelings through printmaking		○	●	●	●	●	●	●	●	●
Create an artwork using a variety of printmaking tools and materials such as tempera or liquid school acrylic, brushes, string, fingers, sponges, found objects, paper		○	●	●	●	●	●	●	●	●
	Sculpture									
Express individual ideas, thoughts, and feelings through sculpture		○	●	●	●	●	●	●	●	●
Understand the differences between two-dimensional artworks and sculpture		○	●	●	●	●	●	●	●	●
Create an artwork using a variety of sculpture tools and materials for sculpture such as papier-mâché, plaster of Paris, kiln-fired clay		○	●	●	●	●	●	●	●	●
Differentiate between additive and subtractive sculpture				○	●	●	●	●	●	●

Scope and Sequence

	Levels								
	K	1	2	3	4	5	6	7	8
Textiles and Fibers									
Express individual ideas, thoughts, and feelings through textiles or fibers	○	●	●	●	●	●	●	●	●
Identify characteristics of fibers in textiles: heavy, light, smooth, rough, natural, synthetic, tightly woven, loosely woven			○	●	●	●	●	●	●
Create a textile artwork using a variety of fiber tools and materials such as yarn, string, plastic, synthetic fabric, natural fabric	○	●	●	●	●	●	●	●	●
Create a textile artwork using a variety of methods: weaving, knotting, batik, stitchery	○	●	●	●	●	●	●	●	●
Technology and Photographic Imagery									
Express individual ideas, thoughts, and feelings through photographic imagery				○	●	●	●	●	●
Create a photographic artwork using a variety of tools and materials such as sun prints, photograms, photomontages				○	●	●	●	●	●
Understand that photographic imagery can be still or motion		○	●	●	●	●	●	●	●
Understand that photographic imagery can be made with a variety of tools and materials such as still cameras, video cameras, motion picture cameras	○	●	●	●	●	●	●	●	●
Explore and examine a variety of ways that computer technology is used to create works of art	○	●	●	●	●	●	●	●	●
Simple Architectural Structures and Environmental Art									
Express individual ideas, thoughts, and feelings through simple architectural structures and environmental art	○	●	●	●	●	●	●	●	●
Recognize simple architectural structures and environmental art	○	●	●	●	●	●	●	●	●
Construct simple architectural models of structures from a variety of materials such as sticks, rocks, bricks, plastic, wood, boxes, fabric	○	●	●	●	●	●	●	●	●
Differentiate among a variety of architectural styles							○	●	●
Recognize how architectural styles relate to environmental factors: cultural traditions, aesthetic values, climates, geographic locations, types of available materials, landscapes					○	●	●	●	●
Sketchbook and Portfolio **Keep a sketchbook to:**									
record own artworks	○	●	●	●	●	●	●	●	●
observe and evaluate development of creativity, originality, and individuality in style	○	●	●	●	●	●	●	●	●
Keep a portfolio to:									
organize own artworks	○	●	●	●	●	●	●	●	●
document, observe, and evaluate artistic development	○	●	●	●	●	●	●	●	●
Safety in the Creative Art Process **Safety**									
Demonstrate a cautious respect for art materials and tools	○	●	●	●	●	●	●	●	●
Demonstrate caring for and cleaning art materials and tools	○	●	●	●	●	●	●	●	●